Selected Sermons
from the Pastoral Epistles

John Calvin

Other Related Titles

In addition to *Selected Sermons from the Pastoral Epistles* Solid Ground Christian Books is delighted to offer the following other volumes related to John Calvin and his ministry.

The Humanness of John Calvin: The Reformer as a Husband, Father, Pastor and Friend by Richard Stauffer

The Word and Prayer: Classic Devotions from the Minor Prophets by John Calvin

Calvin on Scripture and Divine Sovereignty by John Murray

Calvin Memorial Addresses: Celebrating the 400th Anniversary of the Birth of John Calvin in 1909 by Warfield, Orr, Webb et al

Sermons from Job by John Calvin

Sermons on the Saving Work of Christ by John Calvin

Sermons on the Ten Commandments by John Calvin

Selected Sermons
from the Pastoral Epistles

John Calvin

Solid Ground Christian Books
Birmingham, Alabama USA

Solid Ground Christian Books
PO Box 660132
Vestavia Hills AL 35266
205-443-0311
mike.sgcb@gmail.com
www.solid-ground-books.com

SELECTED SERMONS FROM THE PASTORAL EPISTLES
by John Calvin (1509-1564)

Taken from the 1831 edition by *T. Desilver, Jr., Philadelphia*, entitled "A Selection of the Most Celebrated Sermons of John Calvin"

First Solid Ground edition in March 2012

Cover design by Borgo Design
Contact them at borgogirl@bellsouth.net

ISBN- 978-159925-3206

TABLE OF CONTENTS

Biography of John Calvin (Extracted from Mackenzie's *Memoirs of the Life & Writings of Calvin*)	3
SERMON 1 - 1 Timothy 3:16 *"God Was Manifest in the Flesh"*	21
SERMON 2 - 2 Timothy 1:8,9 *"Be Not Ashamed of the Testimony of our Lord"*	34
SERMON 3 - 2 Timothy 1:9,10 *"The Appearing of our Savior Jesus Christ"*	46
SERMON 4 - 2 Timothy 2:16-18 *"Shun Profane and Vain Babblings"*	59
SERMON 5 - Titus 1:15,16 *"To the Defiled and Unbelieving Nothing is Pure"*	72
SERMON 6 - 2 Timothy 2:19 *"The Foundation of God Standeth Sure"*	84
SERMON 7 - 1 Timothy 2:3-5 *"There is One Mediator Between God and Man"*	96
SERMON 8 - 1 Timothy 3:14,15 *"The Pillar and Ground of the Truth"*	111
SERMON 9 - 2 Timothy 3:16,17 *"All Scripture Given By Inspiration of God"*	124
SERMON 10 - 2 Timothy 2:20,21 *"A Vessel Unto Honor"*	137
SERMON 11 - Titus 1:7-9 *"A Bishop Must be Blameless, as the Steward of God"*	150
SERMON 12 - Titus 1:10-12 *"There are Many Unruly and Vain Talkers"*	162
SERMON 13 - 1 Timothy 2:8 *"I Will therefore that Men Pray Everywhere"*	172
SERMON 14 - 1 Timothy 2:5,6 *"The Man Christ Jesus Gave Himself a Ransom"*	185

ADVERTISEMENT.

In offering this selection of Sermons to the publick, the publisher has not been governed by Sectarian principles, but has selected Sermons upon various subjects, that the reader may understand the general doctrine held forth by those eminent divines. When we consider the mental darkness which enveloped the world in the days of Luther and Calvin, under Popish superstition and idolatry, and that theirs were some of the first attempts to emancipate the human intellect from more than "Egyptian darkness," the reader will undoubtedly censure lightly any defects that may appear in their discourses; considering their great object to have been, the removal of that servile yoke of papistry under which *nations* were groaning, and of bringing mankind into the liberty of the gospel.

Calvin's Sermons were translated and published in England, about the year 1580; since which date we have no account of an edition having been published. Luther's Sermons, after having been translated, were published in the year 1581, and re-published in 1649. In consequence of the imperfection of the English Language when these Sermons were formerly published, it was found necessary to revise them, and correct the language; but in so doing, particular care has been taken to preserve precisely the original meaning.

BIOGRAPHY

OF

JOHN CALVIN, D. D.

Extracted from John Mackenzie's Memoirs of the Life and Writings of Calvin.

JOHN CALVIN, the celebrated Reformer, was born at Noyon, a town in Picardy, on the 10th of July, 1509. Undistinguished by the splendour of family consideration, it was reserved for him to give dignity and perpetuity to a name, which had hitherto occupied an humble, but respectable, rank in society. His father, whose name was Gerard, a sensible and prudent man, had gained the esteem and friendship of all the neighbouring gentlemen, and particularly of the family of Montmor, a family of the first distinction in Picardy. John Calvin was brought up with the children of this family, and accompanied them to Paris, where, with them, he pursued his studies under Marturin Cordier, a man illustrious for his erudition and integrity.

His next tutor was a learned Spaniard, under whose tuition he advanced so rapidly, that he soon entered upon the study of philosophy. But as he had from his youth discovered considerable piety, his father thought he should be following the inclination of his son, in consecrating him to theology. He therefore procured for him, in the year 1529, a benefice in the cathedral church at Noyon, where he was born. Here Calvin, though unordained, preached frequently. How little did it appear from Calvin's present situation and prospects, (a member and a minister of the church of Rome,) that he should be an instrument appointed to overthrow that pile of corruption!

Calvin, having been instructed in the true religion by one of his relatives, and having carefully perused the scriptures, began to be disgusted with the church of Rome, and resolved to renounce her communion. His father, in the mean time, resolved to have him study the law, being convinced that it was the most certain method of acquiring riches and honour. Thus, either to comply with his father's wishes, or his own inclination, he quitted the study of theology, for that of the law: he removed to Orleans, where he made such progress in that science, under one of the most celebrated of all the French civilians, that he was considered rather a master than a scholar. In the absence of the professors, he frequently supplied their places, and acquired so much esteem in the university, that he was offered a doctor's degree.

In the midst of his various employments, our reformer was a diligent student of the Holy Scriptures. He was so diligent at this time, that after having supped lightly, he continued reading until midnight; and in the morning was employed, while in bed, in reviewing what he had read the night before. Although these late studies contributed to his extensive erudition, and his remarkable memory, yet they injured his health materially, and brought on that weakness of stomach with which he was afflicted during his life, and which at length shortened his days.

Calvin studied Greek under Melchior Wolmar, a professor of considerable merit, and an excellent tutor. With his laborious studies he associated an incessant perusal of the scriptures, and sometimes preached in a small town in Berri. His father dying, he was obliged to abandon the study of law, and return to Noyon. He visited Paris shortly afterwards, where he published his Commentary on Seneca's Book on Clemency, an author, the purity of whose sentiments were in perfect unison with the morals of Calvin. He was then only twenty-four years of age; but, notwithstanding his youth, he soon became known, and highly esteemed.

During his residence at Paris, renouncing the pursuit of all other sciences, he consecrated himself to theology and to God. While here, having spoken against some public errours in religion, an attempt was made to take him prisoner, but he made his escape by flight. The queen of Navarre, a princess of uncommon merit, having sent for Calvin, treated him with great respect. She made use of her influence with the king, Francis I., her brother, to appease the tempest which had arisen against the reformed. Having quitted Paris, Calvin retired to Xaintonge, where, at the request of a friend, he composed some formularies of sermons and christian exhortations, which he induced the rectors to use as homilies, in order to excite the people to pursue their inquiries into the truth.

Calvin soon returned to Paris, but having many enemies there, who had meditated his destruction, he was obliged to remain concealed. The following year was disgraced by many cruelties inflicted upon several pious characters. The king, Francis I., being influenced by the Catholics, was so highly incensed by some writings which had been published against the Mass, that he commanded eight of the reformed to be burned alive, in the middle of the four most frequented parts of the city; and swore he would not spare his own children, should they be infected with that execrable heresy.

Considering the deplorable state to which his brethren were reduced, Calvin resolved to quit the kingdom. He therefore proceeded to Basil by the way of Lorraine, where he applied himself to the study of the Hebrew language. Though he wished at this time to remain in obscurity, as appears by a letter written to him by Bucer, yet he was constrained to publish his Christian Institutes, to serve as an apology for his persecuted brethren. For as Francis I. was desirous of the friendship of the protestant princes of Germany, and knew that they would disapprove of the murder of his protestant subjects, he affirmed that he had only put to death the Anabaptists, who, far from making the word of God the rule of their faith, gave themselves up to their disordered imaginations, professing a contempt for magistrates and sovereign authorities.

Calvin, who could not bear to see the true religion thus calumniated, thought it necessary to publish his Institutes, which he dedicated to Francis I. While he was finishing this work, he learned that in many places of Italy, ideas were cherished favourable to the Reformation: he therefore flew to the celebrated Dutchess de Ferrare, the daughter of Louis XII., who received him with distinction, and whom Calvin confirmed in her principles. Notwithstanding this protection, the Inquisition, aroused by the name of Calvin, pursued him to the court of the Dutchess, from which he was obliged to make his escape. It was, no doubt, at this time that he arrived at the town of Piedmont, in which he at first preached the Reformation with success; but from whence he was afterwards driven by intolerance. This fact is attested by a pillar of eight feet in height, still existing, erected to immortalize the arrival of Calvin at Aost, and his banishment from thence.

On quitting Italy, Calvin returned to France: but on account of the persecutions which then ran high, he soon resolved to return to Basil or Strasbourg. But the direct road being then impassable on account of the war, he was compelled to go through Geneva. This was in the month of August, 1536. The reformed religion had been wonderfully established there by Guillaume Farel and Pierre Viret. Calvin, not willing to pass through Geneva without paying his respects to them, made them a visit; on which occasion, Farel earnestly entreated him to stop at Geneva, and help him in the labour to which God had called him. Calvin submitted to their wishes, and was received to the charge of the ministry the same month.

From this time, says the Rev. A. Le Mercier, in his Church History of Geneva, " The excellent works, the various circumstances of the life, the great pains, and unwearied industry of this great man, make up a great part of the ecclesiastical history of Geneva, for near thirty years." Soon after Calvin came to Geneva, he engaged in a defence of the reformed, who were attacked by the Anabaptists, against whom he employed scripture and argument with so much success, that he entirely expelled that sect from Geneva. In the same year he was obliged to plead his cause at Bern, against Caroly, who had accused him of Arianism.

Geneva was at this time very far from being in a state of tranquillity, although the true religion was established, and the faith of the church of Rome abolished. Calvin and Farel were hated by those who preferred their vices and pleasures to good order; they therefore united their efforts to get rid of those vigilant ministers. And taking advantage of some disagreements between the church of Bern and that of Geneva, respecting ecclesiastical discipline, they procured an order from the council, by which these faithful ministers were commanded to leave the town in three days. Farel retired to

Neufchatel, and Calvin to Strasbourg; where the council of that town appointed him professor of theology, and pastor of a French church, into which he introduced his ecclesiastical discipline.

Calvin expressed much tenderness toward the Genevese, and took an interest in all their afflictions. He addressed several letters to them from Strasbourg, wherein he exhorted them to repentance, to peace, to charity, and to the love of God; teaching them to hope that a bright light would soon dissipate the fatal darkness in which they were enveloped. The event justified the prediction. At this time he republished his Christian Institutes, with many additions: he also published a piece on the Lord's Supper, which was very much admired. He reclaimed many Anabaptists, who were brought to him from various parts; and amongst others, Paul Volse, who died a minister of Strasbourg, and Jean Storder Liegeois, whose widow Calvin afterwards married, by the advice of Bucer: she was a person of extraordinary merit.

Such were the occupations of Calvin until the year 1541, when the Emperor Charles V. convoked a diet at Worms, and afterwards at Ratisbonne, to settle the differences which had arisen in Germany. Calvin, by desire of the ministers of Strasbourg, assisted at the diet, in which he proved useful to the churches, and particularly to those of France. Philip Melancthon, who always spoke with applause of Calvin, called him *The Theologian*.

The faction which had procured the banishment of Calvin being overthrown, the Genevese were anxious to recal him; but he resisted the offers which they made him. At length, solicited afresh by the council and the ministers of that town, and encouraged by Bucer, who informed him that the council had revoked his banishment, on the 1st of May, 1541, he set out for Geneva, where, upon his arrival, he was congratulated by the acclamations of the people.

Shortly after his return, he composed a catechism in Latin and in French, divided into questions and answers. This work, which proved highly useful to the church, was so well received by different nations, that it was not only translated into many living languages, such as the German, the English, the Flemish, the Spanish, and the Italian, but also into Hebrew and Greek. Notwithstanding the relief which Calvin continually received from Farel and Viret, it is not easy to conceive how he sustained his various labours; especially if we consider that he was the subject of several violent and continual disorders. During a fortnight in each month, he preached every day; gave three lectures in theology every week; assisted at all the deliberations of the Consistory, and at the meetings of the pastors; met the congregation every Friday; instructed the French churches by the frequent advices which they solicited from him; defended the Reformation against the attacks of its enemies, and particularly those of the French priests; was forced to repel his numerous antagonists, by various books which he composed for that purpose; and found time to publish several other works.

In addition to these occupations, the council, who knew that he was an excellent civilian, as well as theologian, consulted him in all important concerns, and charged him with many difficult commissions. He was particularly employed in framing the edicts and legislative acts of the town, which were completed and approved in the year 1543. In this year he presented the church of Geneva with a liturgy, together with directions as to the manner of celebrating the Lord's Supper, and Baptism. Mosheim says, "the senate of that city, by the request of Calvin, established an academy, which contributed much to the success of his designs. He, with his colleague, Theodore Beza, and other divines of eminent learning and abilities, taught the sciences with the greatest reputation. The lustre which these great men reflected upon this infant seminary of learning, spread its fame through the distant nations with such amazing rapidity, that all who were ambitious of a distinguished progress in either sacred or profane erudition, repaired to Geneva. England, Scotland, France, Italy, and Germany, seemed to vie with each other in the number of their students, that were incessantly repairing to the new academy. By these means, and by the ministry of his disciples, Calvin gained proselytes and patrons to his theological system, in several countries of Europe.

In the year 1547, Calvin composed a work entitled *L'Antidote*, against the doctrine contained in the first seven sections of the Council of Trent. He wrote also to the church of Rouen, to fortify her against the artifices and errours of a certain monk of the order of St. Francis, who was endeavouring to infect that church with the heresy of Carpocrates. About this time he composed his commentaries on the Epistles of St. Paul. The church of Geneva, though surrounded by afflictions, increased rapidly ; and Calvin received, with every mark of tenderness, those who were banished from their country on account of their attachment to the gospel. He now met with a severe trial in the loss of his wife, a person of singular virtue and merit ; but though extremely affected by this affliction, he endured it with a constancy and resignation becoming his exalted character.

The churches of Saxony, not being united in some things, consulted Calvin, who frankly gave his opinion on the subject ; and as Melancthon was accused (though unjustly) of too much indifference on this subject, he wrote to him respecting it. While God was on the one hand chastising the German churches with the scourge of discord, he manifested his compassion to the churches of Switzerland; for Calvin and Farel having made a visit to Zurich, composed all the differences which had arisen among them on the subject of the sacraments. Articles were agreed upon by the consent of the churches of Switzerland, and those of the Grisons; and this agreement united the church of Zurich and that of Geneva in the closest bonds.

The ministers of Geneva, in a public assembly, having illustrated and established the doctrine of predestination, approved of the work which Calvin had written on that subject. His writings were already translated into the different languages of Europe; and Geneva was thronged with strangers from Germany, France, Poland, Hungary, and even from Spain and Italy, who came to consult him about the advancement of the Reformation, or to find shelter from the persecutions to which they were exposed in their native countries. Calvin was respected by none more than by the Protestants of England; and by the desire of Archbishop Cranmer, he had imparted to Edward VI. his advice relative to the best method of advancing the Reformation in that kingdom. Knox was affectionately received by Calvin as a refugee from England; and an intimate friendship was soon formed between them, which subsisted until the death of Calvin in 1564.

Calvin, in the case of Servetus, has been harshly censured. It has been confidently pretended, and boldly asserted, that he through life, nourished an implacable hatred against Servetus, and that he employed all his efforts to satiate it in the blood of the unhappy Spaniard. It is certain that Servetus had rendered himself odious to all who knew him, and that the ideas of most persons agreed with those of Calvin on the punishment which he merited. It is evident from the letters of Farel and of Viret, that they did not blame Calvin in this affair. Bucer was not ashamed to write that "Servetus deserved something worse than death." The excellent Melancthon approved the punishment of Servetus. Writing to Calvin, he remarks: "In my opinion, your magistrates have acted justly, in putting to death a blasphemer, convicted by due process of law." Farel expressly says, that "Servetus deserved a capital punishment." And Beza defended the sentence. All these celebrated men entertained the same opinion on this subject; and as no personal hatred of Servetus can be imputed to them, it is at least as unjust to accuse Calvin of it.

Servetus was condemned upon extracts from his books, and from the edition of the Bible which he had published in 1552, and from a letter which he had written to Abel Paupin, a minister of Geneva. The principal accusations exhibited against him were, First, his having asserted that the Bible celebrated improperly the fertility of the land of Canaan, whilst it was unfruitful and barren. Secondly, his having called one God in three persons a Cerberus; a three headed monster. Thirdly, his having taught that God was all, and that all was God. To the council of Geneva, justice ought to be done with respect to this transaction, though we may blame the principles of its jurisprudence: they neglected nothing to discover the truth; they multiplied their interrogatories, and employed all possible means to make Servetus retract: and, as they experienced the inutility of these measures, they wrote to the reformed Swiss cantons for their advice. Is it credible? they were unanimous in exhorting the council to *punish the wicked man, and to put it out of his power to increase heresy.*

If Calvin may be supposed to have influenced the Council of Geneva, can it be said that he controlled the Councils of four different states, and all the persons who were consulted by them, in forming their judgements? Shall the fury imputed to him render so many magistrates cruel, whom he had never known? It must be confessed, that the intolerant spirit of the age dictated the sentence of Servetus at Geneva. On the 27th of October, Servetus was condemned to be burnt alive; and the sentence was executed on the same day.

In the first place, let it be remembered, that the fate of Servetus was approved by the majority of celebrated ecclesiastics among the reformed of those times: it was also sanctioned by the church of Switzerland, who even recommended it. It had long been the custom at Geneva to proceed with violence against heretics. In the year 1536, several persons were deprived of their freedom for not embracing the received doctrine: from the year 1541, the Consistory possessed the right of forcing the magistrates and the people to continue faithful to the holy doctrine, and to observe good morals.

In 1558, Gentilis escaped death only by retraction, though it was known to be feigned: and Calvin, in a letter which he wrote at that time, observed, "Servetus, by a recantation, might have averted his punishment: I would have it attested that my hostility was not so deadly; but that by humility alone, had he not been deprived of his senses, he might have saved his life; but I know not how to account for his conduct, without supposing him to have been seized with a fatal insanity, and to have plunged himself headlong into ruin."

The civil and ecclesiastical jurisprudence of the tribunals with respect to heresy, was undoubtedly grossly inconsistent with the spirit of christianity, and the principles of equity. But if we could transport ourselves into that age, and contemplate the circumstances in which Calvin was placed, divesting our minds of prejudice, we should no doubt perceive that the sentence was that of the civil judges, and that they strictly followed the ordinary course of the law; that Calvin followed the judgement of all the ecclesiastics of his time, and complied with the sanguinary laws of every country in Europe against heretics.

It cannot, however, be denied, that in this instance Calvin acted contrary to the benignant spirit of the gospel. It is better to drop a tear over the inconsistency of human nature, and to bewail those infirmities which cannot be justified. He declares he acted conscientiously, and publickly justified the act.

Calvin, being convinced that the best method to preserve the purity of religion was to enlighten men's understandings, used his utmost exertions to found a college, in which youth might be well instructed. In the year 1556, he proposed the establishment of one; but foreign affairs prevented the Council from attending to the object at that time. At length, in the year 1559, he had the satisfaction of seeing his wishes accomplished; a college being founded, and furnished with enlightened teachers: an academy was also erected, which acquired the esteem of foreigners by the celebrity of its professors.

Calvin was this year attacked with a quartan ague, which laid the foundation of his subsequent illness and death; for though he recovered his health eight months afterwards, he was so much reduced as never again to be perfectly restored. During his illness, he used to remark, that idleness was extremely irksome to him. About this time he revised and republished his Institutes, in Latin and in French; and corrected his Commentaries on

Isaiah, in such a manner as to render it a new work.

The Catholics at this time had obtained an entire influence over Henry II, and abused his compliance by exciting a persecution against the Protestants. With this view, they induced that prince to publish several severe edicts against them, and to imprison some of the counsellors of the parliament of Paris, who were suspected of favouring their cause; and inspired him with the design of destroying the *New Sect*—a name by which they were then called. But while the church was overwhelmed with consternation, Henry II was mortally wounded at a tournament, by one of his captains of the guards, who, by his orders, had a few days before arrested the counsellors: this event changing the face of affairs, the reformed were delivered from a danger which appeared inevitable.

After the death of Henry II, Calvin was accused of having raised a conspiracy against Francis II, although he had disapproved of the enterprise, and employed his efforts to subdue it. After the death of Francis II, Charles IX wrote to the Council of Geneva in 1561, to complain of their receiving into the town the enemies of France, and fostering those public disturbers. Calvin was accordingly summoned, with his colleagues, before the Council; and admitted that the pastors had sent into France several pious men, to regulate the churches there, which they had been solicited to do; but that they were too deeply occupied about the advancement of religion to be employed in sowing troubles in the kingdom; and that he was ready, with his colleagues, to answer their accusers before the king. Charles acknowledged apparently the innocence of Calvin and his colleagues, for nothing farther was heard upon the subject.

Soon afterwards, Calvin published a work showing the errours with which the work of Gentilis, against the Creed of Athanasius, was filled. He also published at this time his work on Daniel, which he dedicated to the churches of France. The disputes in which Calvin was interested were not yet finished: in 1561, a fresh discussion arose between him and Baldwin, who had published, during the conference of Poissy, a book of Cassander's: to this work Calvin replied; a controversy ensued, in the course of which a warmth of temper was betrayed on both sides, which reflected no honour on the disputants; but which is far from being singular in theological controversies.

The disorders of Calvin were visibly increasing, and it was evident that he was making rapid advances toward another world. His afflictions, however weighty, never dejected him. His usual duties of visiting the sick and afflicted, of preaching and giving theological lectures, were punctually discharged: and knowing that the churches of France were not only openly attacked, but secretly defamed to the German princes, he drew up their confession of faith, which was presented to the Diet of Frankfort.

Calvin's disorders were still growing worse, which rendered his exertions at this period almost incredible; for notwithstanding his reduced state, he could not be induced to remit, in the slighest degree, his ordinary occupations. Amongst his numerous avocations at this time, were the exhortations which he gave on the subject of the Holy Trinity; his answers to the deputies of the Synod of Lyons; the Commentaries which he composed in French and in Latin, upon the Books of Moses; as well as his Commentary upon the Book of Joshua, which he began this year, and finished a little before his death.

The year 1564, occasioned a deep and lasting grief to Geneva. On the second of February he delivered his last sermon, and on the same day, his last theological lecture. His asthma deprived him of the use of his voice, and he abstained from all the functions of his charge. He was sometimes carried to the congregation, but seldom spoke.

In a letter which he wrote to the physicians, he gave an account of the maladies which his various labours of body and mind had brought upon him. For, besides being of a dry and feeble temperament, and strongly inclined to consumption, he slept very unsoundly. During ten years, at least, he ate no dinner, taking no nourishment until supper-time. He was subject to a head-ache, the only remedy for which was fasting; on account of which he sometimes remained thirty-six hours without eating. He was also frequently attacked by the hemorrhoids, which were brought on partly by his efforts in preaching, and partly by the excessive use of aloes: and five years before his death he was seized with a spitting of blood.

After Calvin was cured of the quartan ague, he was attacked by the gout: he was afterwards afflicted with the colick, and a few months before his death, with the stone. The physicians exhausted their art upon him, and no man ever observed their instructions with more regularity. But as to what relates to the labours of the mind, he had so little respect to his health, that the most violent headaches never prevented his appearance in the pulpit in his turn. Afflicted as he was by so many maladies, he was never known to pronounce a word unworthy of a christian, or of a man of constancy and courage. In his greatest agonies, lifting his eyes to heaven, he was accustomed to repeat the words, "How long, O Lord!" When in health, he frequently made use of these words, with reference to the calamities of his brethren in Jesus Christ, whose afflictions were much more painful to him than his own.

Calvin having been informed by a letter from Farel, that, though he was eighty-four years of age, and loaded with infirmities, he had resolved to visit him; replied, "I wish you perfect health, my very dear brother; and since God intends you should remain in this world after me, remember ever our union, which hath produced so many advantages to the church, and the fruit of which we shall gather in heaven. I beg, however, that you would not on my account expose yourself to the fatigue of a journey. My respiration is difficult, and I am about to breathe the last gasp, happy to live and die in Jesus Christ, who is gain to all his children in life and in death; I bid you, and all my brethren, my last adieu."

On the day of his death, which was the 24th of May, he appeared to speak with less difficulty, and more strength. But it was the last effort of nature. About eight o'clock in the evening, the signs of death appeared suddenly in his face; he continued speaking, however, with great propriety, until his last breath, when he appeared rather to fall asleep than die.

On the day following, the whole city was plunged into the most inconceivable grief; for the republick regretted the wisest of its citizens; the church its faithful pastor, and the school its incomparable master. Many ran in crowds to his room, and could scarcely be persuaded to separate themselves from his body. Calvin, after having been concerned in the establishment of many churches in France, Germany, England, and Poland, and having committed his flock, as well as pupils, to his friend and disciple Theodore Beza, closed his indefatigable career; and left behind him in the city which had been the principal theatre of his exertions, a reputation for piety, learning, and wisdom, which has fallen to the lot of scarcely any among his fellow-labourers.

On Sunday, the day after his death, about eight o'clock in the morning, his body was covered and enclosed in a wooden coffin; and at two o'clock in the afternoon he was conveyed, without any pomp, to the common burying place, called Plein Palais. The ministers, professors, and almost all the inhabitants of the town, attended at the funeral ceremony with expressions of the deepest grief. No inscription was put upon his tomb, because he had expressly forbidden it; but the following elegant epigram was written by his friend Beza.

> Shall honour'd Calvin to the dust return,
> From whom e'en Virtue's self might virtue learn;
> Shall he—of falling Rome the greatest dread,
> By all the good bewailed, and now (tho' dead)
> The terrour of the vile—lie in so mean,
> So small a tomb, where not his name is seen?
> Sweet Modesty, who still by Calvin's side
> Walk'd while he liv'd, here laid him when he died.
> O happy tomb with such a tenant graced!
> O envied marble o'er *his* ashes placed!

Calvin was fifty-four years old when he died, half of which time he spent in the labours of the ministry. He was of the middle size, a pale face, brown complexion, and brilliant eyes, which announced the penetration and vivacity of his mind. Neat and modest in his habits, as well as moderate in his eating, he had no less horrour of luxury than of impurity. He ate, indeed, so little, that during several years he partook of only one meal a day, on account of the weakness of his stomach. He slept but little. Being of a bilious habit, he was easily excited to choler, a susceptibility considerably increased by a studious and laborious life.

Though Calvin was sufficiently attached to his own opinions, he respected those of others; and though fixed in his sentiments, he knew how to esteem and commend those who did not hold, and even those who condemned them. It is well known that he was thoroughly decided on the doctrine of predestination; he, however, translated into French, the *Sum of Theology*, by Melancthon, who was considerably more reserved on this subject than Calvin. In a preface which Calvin wrote to that work, he described with energy the disputes so ill managed on those subjects; saying, that "they were perplexed and confused, and produced no fruit of profitable instruction."

When it is recollected that the writings of Calvin fill twenty folio volumes; that he maintained a constant and extensive correspondence on the subject of the Reformation, and the state of the Protestant churches; and that he was continually employed in preaching—in giving theological lectures—and in assisting at all the deliberations of the Consistory; it might be supposed, as has been observed, that his "soul of fire" must have been supported by "a frame of adamant." Had he anticipated eternal life, as the wages of laborious piety, he could not have exemplified a more blameless life; but he looked for it, as "the gift of God through Jesus Christ our Lord."

CALVIN'S SERMONS.

SERMON I.

I Timothy, Chap. iii. *verse* 16.

16 And without controversy great is the mystery of godliness; God was manifest in the flesh, justified in the Spirit, seen of angels, preached unto the Gentiles, believed on in the world, received up into glory.

WE noticed in the morning how St. Paul exhorted Timothy to behave himself in his office; showing him to what honour God had advanced him, in that he had placed him to govern his house. He showed him also that the office itself was honourable; because the church upholdeth the truth of God in this world, and that there is nothing more precious, or more to be sought after, than to know God, and to worship and serve him, and be certain of his truth, that we might thereby obtain salvation. All this is kept safe for us: and thus, so great a treasure is committed to our care by means of the church; according to the words of St. Paul. This truth is well worthy to be more highly esteemed than it is.

What a hidden thing is this, and how wonderful a matter; that God was manifest in the flesh, and became man! does it not so far surpass our understanding, that when we are told of it, we are astonished? Yet notwithstanding, we have a full and sufficient proof, that Jesus Christ being made man, and subject to death, is likewise the true God, who made the world, and liveth forever. Of this, his heavenly power beareth us witness. Again, we have other proofs: to wit, he was preached unto the Gentiles; who before were banished from the kingdom of God: and that faith hath had its course throughout the whole world, which at that time was shut up among the Jews; and likewise Christ Jesus was lifted up on high, and entered into glory; and sitteth on the right hand of God the Father.

If men despise these things, their unthankfulness shall be condemned: for the very angels have hereby come to the knowledge of that which before they knew not of. For it pleased God to hide the means of our redemption from them, to the end that his goodness might be so much the more wonderful to all creatures: thus we see St. Paul's meaning. He calleth the church of God, the keeper of his truth: he likewise showeth that this truth is such a treasure, as ought to be highly esteemed by us. And why so? let us mark the contents of the gospel; God abased himself in such a manner, that he took upon himself our flesh; so that we have become his brethren. Who is the Lord of glory, that he should so far humble himself, as to be joined to us, and take upon him the form of a servant, even to suffer the curse that was due to us? St. Paul comprehendeth all things whatsoever that Jesus Christ received in his person; to wit, that he was subject to all our infirmities, *sin only excepted.*

It is true that there is no blemish in him, but all pureness and perfection. Yet so it is, that he became weak as we are, that he might have compassion and help our feebleness; as it is set forth in the epistle to the Hebrews, chap. iv. 15. He that had no sin suffered the punishment due to us; and was, as it were, accursed of God the Father, when he offered himself a sacrifice; that through his means we might be blessed; and that his grace which was hidden from us, might be poured upon us. When we consider these things, have we not occasion to be astonished? Do we consider what a being God is?

We can in no wise reach unto his majesty, which containeth all things in itself; which even the angels worship.

What is there in us? If we cast our eyes upon God, and then enter into a comparison, alas! shall we come near this highness which surmounteth the heavens? Nay, rather can we have any acquaintance with it? For there is nothing but rottenness in us; nothing but sin and death. Then let the living God, the well-spring of life, the everlasting glory, and the infinite power, come; and not only approach to us and our miseries, our wretchedness, our frailty, and to this bottomless pit of all iniquity that is in men; let not only the majesty of God come near this, but be joined to it, and made one with it, in the person of our Lord Jesus Christ! What is Jesus Christ? God and man! But how God and man? what difference is there between God and man?

We know that there is nothing at all in our nature but wretchedness and misery; nothing but a bottomless pit of stench and infection; and yet in the person of our Lord Jesus Christ, we see the glory of God who is worshipped by angels, and likewise the weakness of man; and that he is God and man. Is not this a secret and hidden thing, worthy to be set out with words, and likewise enough to ravish our hearts! The very angels could never have thought upon it, as here observed by St. Paul. Seeing it pleased the Holy Ghost to set forth the goodness of God, and show us for how precious a jewel we ought to esteem it, let us beware on our part that we be not unthankful, and have our minds so shut up, that we will not taste of it, if we cannot thoroughly and perfectly understand it.

It is enough for us to have some little knowledge of this subject; each one ought to be content with what light is given him, considering the weakness of our judgement; and looking for the day wherein that which we now see in part, shall be wholly and perfectly revealed to us. Yet notwithstanding, we must employ our minds and studies this way. Why doth St. Paul call this a mystery of faith, that Jesus Christ, who is God everlasting, was manifest in the flesh? It is as much as if he should say, when we are gathered to God, and made one body with the Lord Jesus Christ, we shall behold the end for which we were made ; to wit, that we might know that God is joined and made one with us in the person of his Son.

Thus, we must conclude that no man can be a christian, unless he know this secret which is spoken of by St. Paul. Should we now examine, and ask both men and women whether they know what these words mean, that God was manifest in the flesh, scarcely one in ten could make so good an answer as would be looked for from a child. And yet we need not marvel at it; for we see what negligence and contempt there is in the greatest part of mankind. We show and teach daily in our sermons, that God took upon him our nature: but how do men hear them ? Who is there that troubleth himself much to read the scripture ? There are very few that attend to these things ; every man is occupied with his own business.

If there be one day in the week reserved for religious instruction, when they have spent six days in their own business, they are apt to spend the day which is set apart for worship, in play and pastime ; some rove about the fields, others go to the taverns to quaff: and there are undoubtedly at this time as many at the last mentioned place, as are here assembled in the name of God. Therefore, when we see so many shun and flee from this doctrine, can we marvel that there is such a brutishness, that we know not the rudiments of christianity ? We are apt to consider it as a strange language, when men tell us that God was manifest in the flesh.

But this sentence cannot be put out of God's register. We have no faith, if we know not that our Lord Jesus Christ is joined to us, that we may become his members. It seemeth that God would stir us up to think upon this mystery, seeing we are so sleepy and drowsy. We see how the devil stirreth up these old makebates to deny the humanity of Jesus Christ, and his Godhead: and sometimes to confound them both; that we may not perceive two distinct natures in him: or else to cause us to believe that he is not the man who fulfilled the promises in the law; and consequently descended from the stock of Abraham and David.

Is it indeed the case, that such errours and heresies as were in the church of Christ at the beginning, are set forth in these days? Let us mark well the words that are here used by St. Paul: God was manifest in the flesh. When he calleth Jesus Christ God, he admits this nature which he had before the world was made. It is true, there is but one God, but in this one essence we must comprehend the Father, and a wisdom which cannot be severed from him, and an everlasting virtue, which always was, and shall forever be in him.

Thus, Jesus Christ was true God! as he was the wisdom of God before the world was made, and before everlastingness. It is said, he was made manifest in the flesh. By the word *flesh*, St. Paul gives us to understand that he was true man, and took upon him our nature. By the word *manifest*, he showeth that in him there were two natures. But we must not think that there is one Jesus Christ which is God, and another Jesus Christ which is man! but we must know him only as God and man. Let us so distinguish the two natures which are in him, that we may know that the Son of God is our brother.

God suffereth the old heresies, which in times past troubled the church, to make a stir again in our days, to stir us up to diligence. The devil goeth about to destroy this article of our belief, knowing it to be the main prop and stay of our salvation.

If we have not this knowledge of which St. Paul speaketh, what will become of us? We are all Adam's children; and therefore accursed: we are in the bottomless pit of death. There is nothing but death and condemnation in us, until we know that God came down to seek and save us. Until we are thus learned, we are weak and miserable. Therefore, the devil went about doing all in his power to abolish this knowledge, to mar it, and mix it with lies, that he might utterly bring it to nought. When we see such a majesty in God, how dare we presume to come nigh him, seeing we are full of misery! We must have recourse to this *link* of God's majesty, and the state of man's nature together.

Do what we can, we shall never have any hope, or be able to lay hold of the bounty and goodness of God, to return to him, and call upon him, until we know the majesty of God that is in Jesus Christ; and likewise the weakness of man's nature, which he hath received of us. We are utterly cast off from the kingdom of heaven, the gate is shut against us, so that we cannot enter therein. The devil hath bestowed all his art to pervert this doctrine; seeing that our salvation is grounded thereon. We should therefore be so much the more confirmed and strengthened in it; that we may never be shaken, but stand steadfast in the faith, which is contained in the gospel.

First of all we have this to note, that we shall never know Jesus Christ to be our Saviour, until we know that he was God from everlasting. That which was written of him by Jeremiah the prophet, must needs be fulfilled: chap. ix. 24. "Let him that glorieth, glory in this, that he understandeth and knoweth me, that I am the Lord." St. Paul showeth that this must be applied to the person of our Lord Jesus Christ: and thereupon he protesteth that he made no account of any doctrine or knowledge, only to know Jesus Christ.

Again, how is it possible for us to have our life in him, unless he be our God, and we be maintained and preserved by his virtue? How can we put our trust in him? for it is written, Jer. xvii. 5. " Cursed be the man that trusteth in man, and maketh flesh his arm." Again, how can we be preserved from death except by God's infinite power? Although the scriptures bear no record of the Godhead of Christ Jesus, it is impossible for us to know him as our Saviour, unless we admit that he possesses the whole majesty of God; unless we acknowledge him to be the true God; because he is the wisdom of the Father whereby the world was made, preserved, and kept in being. Therefore let us be thoroughly resolved in this point, whenever we speak of Jesus Christ, that we lift our thoughts on high, and worship this majesty which he had from everlasting, and this infinite essence which he enjoyed before he clothed himself in humanity.

Christ was made manifest in the flesh: that is to say, became man; like unto us in all things, sin only excepted: Heb. iv. 15. Where he saith, sin only excepted, he meaneth that our Lord Jesus was without fault or blemish. Yet notwithstanding, he refused not to bear our sins; he took this burden upon himself, that we through his grace might be disburdened. We cannot know Jesus Christ to be a mediator between God and man, unless we behold him as man. When St. Paul would imbolden us to call upon God in the name of our Lord Jesus Christ, he expressly calleth him man.

St. Paul saith, 1 Tim. ii. 5. " There is one God, and one mediator between God and men, the man

Christ Jesus." Under this consideration, we may in his name, and by his means come familiarly to God, knowing that we are his brethren, and he the son of God. Seeing there is nothing but sin in mankind, we must also find righteousness and life in our flesh. Therefore if Christ has not truly become our brother, if he has not been made man like unto us, in what condition are we? Let us now consider his life and passion.

It is said, Hebrews ix. 26. (speaking of Christ,) " But now once in the end of the world hath he appeared, to put away sin by the sacrifice of himself." And why so? St. Paul showeth us the reason in Romans v. 18. " As by the offence of one judgement came upon all men to condemnation; even so by the righteousness of one the free gift came upon all men unto justification of life." If we know not this, that the sin which was committed in our nature, was repaired in the self-same nature, in what situation are we? upon what foundation can we stay ourselves? Therefore, the death of our Lord Jesus Christ could not profit us one whit, unless he had been made man, like unto us.

Again, if Jesus Christ were only God, could we have any certainty or pledge in his resurrection? that we should one day rise again? It is true that the Son of God rose again: when we hear it said, that the Son of God took upon him a body like unto ours, came of the stock of David, that he is risen again, (seeing our nature is of itself corruptible,) and is lifted up on high into glory, in the person of our Lord Jesus Christ, "we are made to sit together in heavenly places in Christ Jesus." Eph. ii. 6. Therefore, those that went about to bring to nought man's nature, in the person of the Son of God, are to be the more detested. For the devil raised up in old times, some individuals, who declared that Jesus Christ appeared in the shape of man, but had not man's true nature : thereby endeavouring to abolish God's mercy towards us, and utterly destroy our faith.

Others have imagined that he brought a body with him from heaven ; as though he partook not of our nature. This was declared by that detestable heretick, (who was here put to death,) that Jesus Christ had a body from everlasting ; composed of four elements : that the Godhead was at that time in a visible shape, and that whenever the angels appeared, it was his body. What madness it is to make such an alchymy, to frame a body for the Son of God ! What shall we do with that passage which saith, Heb. ii. 16, 17. " He took not on him the nature of angels, but he took on him the seed of Abraham. Wherefore in all things it behooved him to be made like unto his brethren, that he might be a merciful and faithful high priest in things pertaining to God, to make reconciliation for the sins of the people."

It is said, he took upon him our flesh, and became our brother. Yea, and that he was made like unto us, that he might have pity upon us, and help our infirmities. He was made the seed of David, that he might be known as the redeemer that was promised? whom the fathers looked for from all ages. Let us remember that it is written, the Son of God appeared in the flesh ; that is, he became very man, and made us one with himself ; so that we may now call God our father. And why so? because we are of the body of his only son. But how are we of his body ? because he was pleased to join himself to us, that we might be partakers of his substance.

Hereby we see that it is not a vain speculation, when men tell us that Jesus Christ put on our flesh: for hither we must come, if we will have a true knowledge of faith. It is impossible for us to trust in him aright, unless we understand his manhood : we must also know his majesty, before we can trust in him for salvation. We must know moreover that Jesus Christ is *God* and *man*, and likewise that he is but one person.

Here again the devil tries to stir up the coals of strife, by perverting or disguising the doctrine which St. Paul teacheth us. For there have been hereticks, who have endeavoured to maintain that the majesty and Godhead of Jesus Christ, his heavenly essence, was forthwith changed into flesh and manhood. Thus did some say, with many other cursed blasphemies, that Jesus Christ was made man. What will follow hereupon? God must forego his nature, and his spiritual essence must be turned into flesh. They go on further, and say, Jesus Christ is no more man, but his flesh has become God.

These are marvellous alchymists, to make so many new natures of Jesus Christ. Thus, the devil raised up such dreamers, in old times, to trouble the faith of the church; who are now renewed in our time. Therefore, let us mark well what St. Paul teaches us in this place; for he giveth us good armour, that we may defend ourselves against such errours. If we would behold Jesus Christ in his true character, let us view in him this heavenly glory, which he had from everlasting: and then let us come to his manhood, which has been described heretofore; that we may distinguish his two natures. This is necessary, to nourish our faith

If we seek life in Jesus Christ, we must understand that he hath the whole Godhead in him; for it is written, Psalm xxxvi. 9. "For with thee is the fountain of life: in thy light shall we see light." If we would be maintained against the devil, and withstand the temptations of our enemies, we must know that Jesus Christ is God. To be short, if we would put our whole trust and confidence in him, we must know that he possesses all power; which he could not have, unless he were God. Who is he that hath all power? It is he that became feeble and weak; the son of the virgin Mary; he that was subject to death; he that bore our sins: he it is, that is the well-spring of life.

We have two eyes in our head, each performing its office: but when we look steadfastly upon a thing, our sight, which is separate of itself, is joined together, and becometh one; and is wholly occupied in beholding that which is set before us: even so are there two diverse natures in Jesus Christ. Is there any thing in the world more different than the body and soul of man? His soul is an invisible spirit that cannot be seen or touched; which hath none of these fleshly passions. The body is a corruptible lump, subject to rottenness; a visible thing which can be touched: the body has its properties, which are entirely different from that of the soul. And thus we ask, what is man? A creature, formed of *body* and *soul.*

If God used such a workmanship in us, when he made us of two diverse natures, why should we think it strange, that he used a far greater miracle in Jesus Christ? St. Paul uses these words, *was manifest,* that we may distinguish his Godhead from his manhood; that we may receive him, as God manifest in the flesh; that is to say, him, who is truly God, and yet hath made himself one with us: therefore we are the children of God; he being our justification, we are delivered from the burden of our sins. Seeing he hath cleansed us from all our misery, we have perfect riches in him; in short, seeing he submitted himself to death, we are now sure of life.

St. Paul addeth, "He was justified in the spirit." The word *justified,* is oftentimes used in scripture, for *approved.* When it is said, he was justified, it is not that he became just, it is not that he was acquitted by men, as though they were his judges, and he bound to give them an account: no, no; there is no such thing; but it is when the glory is given him which he deserveth, and we confess him to be what indeed he really is. It is said, the gospel is justified when men receive it obediently, and through faith submit themselves to the doctrine that God teacheth: so in this place, it is said, Jesus Christ was justified in spirit.

We must not content ourselves by looking at the bodily presence of Jesus Christ, which was visible, but we must look higher. St. John says, chap. i. God was made flesh; or the word of God, which is the same. The word of God, which was God before the creation of the world, was made flesh; that is, was united to our nature: so that the son of the virgin Mary, is God; yea, the everlasting God! His infinite power was there manifested; which is a sure witness that he is the true God! St. Paul saith, Romans i. Jesus Christ our Lord was made of the seed of David; he likewise adds, he was declared to be the Son of God.

It is not enough for us to behold him with our natural eyes; for in this case, we should rise no higher than man: but when we see, that by miracles and mighty works, he showeth himself to be the Son of God, it is a seal and proof, that in abasing himself, he did not leave off his heavenly majesty! Therefore, we may come to him as our brother: and at the same time worship him as the everlasting God; by whom we were made, and by whom we are preserved.

Were it not for this, we could have no church; were it not for this, we could have no religion; were it not for this, we could have no salvation. It would be better for us to be brute beasts, without reason and understanding, than to be destitute of this knowledge: to wit, that Jesus came and joined his Godhead with our nature; which was so wretched and miserable. St. Paul declares this to be a mystery;

that we may not come to it proudly and arrogantly, as many do who wish to be thought wise; this has caused many heresies to spring up. And indeed, pride hath always been the mother of heresies.

When we hear this word, *mystery*, let us remember two things; first, that we learn to keep under our senses, and flatter not ourselves that we have sufficient knowledge and ability to comprehend so vast a matter. In the second place, let us learn to climb up beyond ourselves, and reverence that majesty which passeth our understanding. We must not be sluggish nor drowsy; but think upon this doctrine, and endeavour to become instructed therein. When we have acquired some little knowledge thereof, we should strive to profit thereby, all the days of our life.

When we become possessed of this knowledge, that the Son of God is joined to us, we should cast our eyes upon that which is so highly set forth in him; that is, the virtue and power of the Holy Ghost. So then, Jesus Christ did not only appear as man, but showed indeed that he was Almighty God! as all the fulness of the Godhead dwelt in him. If we once know this, we may well perceive, that it is not without cause that St. Paul saith, all the treasures of wisdom are hidden in our Lord Jesus Christ.

When we have once laid hold on the promises of this mediator, we shall know the height and depth, the length and breadth, yea, and whatsoever is necessary for our salvation: so that we may stay our faith upon him, as upon the only true God; and likewise behold him as our brother; who hath not only come near to us, but hath united and joined himself to us in such a manner, that he hath become the same substance. If we have come to this, let us know that we have arrived to the perfection of wisdom, which is spoken of by St. Paul in another place;

that we may fully rejoice in the goodness of God; for it hath pleased him to lighten us with the brightness of his gospel, and to draw us into his heavenly kingdom.

SERMON II.

2 Timothy, Chap. i. verses 8 and 9.

8 Be not thou therefore ashamed of the testimony of our Lord, nor of me his prisoner: but be thou partaker of the afflictions of the gospel, according to the power of God;
9 Who hath saved us, and called us with an holy calling, not according to our works, but according to his own purpose and grace, which was given us in Christ Jesus before the world began.

Although God shows his glory and majesty in the gospel, yet the unthankfulness of men is such, that we have need to be exhorted, not to be ashamed of this gospel. And why so? because God requires all creatures to do him homage: yet the greater part rebel against him; despise, yea, and are at defiance with the doctrine whereby he would be known and worshipped. Although men are so wicked as to lift up themselves against their maker, let us, notwithstanding, remember that which is taught us in this place; to wit, that we be not ashamed of the gospel; for it is the witness of God.

If the gospel be not preached, Jesus Christ is, as it were, buried. Therefore, let us stand as witnesses, and do him this honour, when we see all the world so far out of the way; and remain steadfast in this wholesome doctrine. St. Paul here setteth his own person before us: not that he wished particularly to be approved, but because we often get in difficulty, if we separate ourselves from the servants of God. When there is a minister of the word of God troubled, molested, and persecuted, we are apt to forsake him in time of need, thinking it is but mortal man: but in doing this, we offend God; because this man that suffereth, beareth the mark of the gospel: thus the cause of God is betrayed. Therefore, St. Paul saith to Timothy, be not ashamed of me.

The mind of Timothy might have been shaken; therefore, St. Paul saith to him, though the world despise me, though they mock and hate me, yet must thou not be moved by these things; for I am the prisoner of Jesus Christ. Let the world speak evil of me; it is not for my offences: God alloweth my cause; for indeed it is his. I suffer not for mine own evil doings, having his truth always on my side. Therefore, the cause of my persecution is, because I have maintained the word of God, and continue to maintain it. Thou shouldst not be guided by the world's judgement, for men are carried away with evil affections. Let it be sufficient for thee then, that I am as it were a pledge for the Son of God; that he magnifieth my person; that if it be reproachful to the world, it ceases not to be honoured before God, and his holy angels.

Let us not deceive Jesus Christ in the testimony we owe him, by stopping our mouths, when it is needful to maintain his honour, and the authority of his gospel. Yea, and when we see our brethren afflicted for the cause of God, let us join with them, and assist them in their affliction. Let us not be shaken by the tempests that arise, but let us always remain constant in our purpose; and stand as witnesses for the Son of God, seeing he is so gracious as to use us in such a good cause. Let us mark well, whether men suffer for their sins, or for the truth of God. When we see one oppressed, we must not despise him, lest we do injury to God: we must ascertain for what cause men suffer. If they have walked in a good conscience, and are blamed, if they are tormented because they serve God, this is enough to remove whatever the wicked world can say against them. Therefore St. Paul adds, "Be thou partaker of the afflictions of the gospel."

There is no man but what would willingly escape affliction; this is according to human nature; and although we confess, without dissembling, that it is a singular grace which God bestows, when he enables men to bear affliction, and maintain his cause, yet there is not one of us, but what would willingly draw his neck out of persecution. For we look not at the lesson given by St. Paul, which saith, the gospel bringeth troubles. Jesus Christ was crucified in his own person, and his doctrine is joined with many miseries. He could, if it pleased him, cause his doctrine to be received without any gainsaying. But the scripture must be fulfilled: "he will rule in the midst of his enemies." Psalm cx.

We must come to him upon this condition; to be willing to suffer many bickerings; because the wicked lift up themselves against God, when he calleth them to him. Therefore, it is impossible for us to have the gospel without affliction. We must be exercised; we must fight under our Lord Jesus Christ. Doth he not then renounce his salvation, that would get rid of the cross of Christ? What is the hope of life, only in this, that we are bought by the sacrifice of the Son of God? Then will he have us made like unto him, and have us transformed into his image.

We must not be ashamed of our brethren; when we hear evil reports of them, and see them cast off by the world, let us always be with them, and endeavour to strengthen them; for the gospel cannot be without affliction; as I have already said. It pleaseth God, that men should be so divided. But he calleth all to the unity of faith; and the doctrine of the gospel is the message of atonement; but yet the faithful are drawn by the virtue of his Holy Spirit; (as we shall notice more particularly hereafter;) but the unbelievers remain in their hardness: thus the fire kindleth; as when thunder engendereth in the air, there must needs be trouble; so it is when the gospel is preached.

Now, if the gospel bring affliction, and it be the mind of Jesus Christ, that what he suffered in his person, shall be fulfilled in his members, and be daily crucified, is it lawful for us to withdraw ourselves from that situation? Seeing it is so, that all hope of salvation is in the gospel, we must rest thereon; and mark what St. Paul saith; to wit, we must assist our brethren when we see them in trouble, and when they are reviled by the wicked; and choose rather to be their companions, and suffer the rebukes and scoffs of the world, than to be otherwise honoured with a good reputation, having our faces turned from them that suffer for that cause, which is ours, as well as theirs.

We are apt to be weak, and think we shall be swallowed up by persecutions, as soon as our enemies assail us: but St. Paul observes, we shall not be destitute of the aid and succour of our God. He armeth us forthwith, and giveth us an invincible power, that we may remain sure and steadfast. For this reason St. Paul adds, "according to the power of God." But as we have said, every man would be glad to have some cover or cloak, whereby he might withdraw himself from persecution. If God would give me grace, I would gladly suffer for his name; I know it is the greatest blessing that I could receive.

Every man will confess this; but they add, we are weak, and shall quickly be beaten down by the cruelty of our enemies. But St. Paul taketh away this excuse, by saying, God will strengthen us, and that we must not look to our own strength. For it is certain, if we never come into conflicts with our enemies, we shall be afraid of our own shadows. Seeing we know this weakness, let us come to the remedy. We must consider how hard it is to withstand our enemies; therefore let us humble ourselves before God, and pray him to extend his hand, and uphold us in all our afflictions. If this doctrine were well imprinted in our hearts, we should be better prepared to suffer than we are.

But we are apt to forget it; yea, we stop our ears, and close our eyes, when we hear it spoken of. We pretend that we wish God to strengthen us, but we cannot bring our sight to the power that St. Paul speaks of; we are apt to think, that we have nothing to do with it; although the Lord hath shown us, that his power shall always uphold us. Therefore, let not our weakness cause us to withdraw ourselves from the cross, and from persecution; seeing God hath received us into his hands, and promised to supply our wants. St. Paul here addeth a lesson to make us greatly ashamed, if we be not enticed to glorify Jesus Christ by suffering persecution; he saith, "God hath saved us, and called us with an holy calling."

Behold! God hath drawn us out of the gulf of hell! We were utterly cast away and condemned: but he hath brought us salvation, and hath called us to be partakers of it. Therefore, seeing God hath showed himself so liberal, if we on our parts turn our backs to him, is not this a shameful malice? Let us mark well the accusation of St. Paul against those that are inconstant; those that are unwilling to suffer the assaults made against them for the sake of the gospel. Undoubtedly his mind was to comfort the faithful, for the time to come; he therefore showeth what God hath done for them already.

When God giveth us any token of his goodness, it is to the end we should hope for the like at his hands again; and wait till he bring to pass what he hath begun. Therefore, if God hath saved us, and called us with an holy calling, do we think that he will leave us at midway? When he hath showed us our salvation, and given us his gospel whereby he calleth us to his kingdom, and openeth the gates unto us; when he hath done all this, do we think he will leave us here, and mock us, and deprive us of his grace, or make it unprofitable? No, no; but let us hope that he will bring his work to a perfect end.

Therefore, let us go on with good courage; for God hath already displayed his power toward us. Let us not doubt but what he will continue it, and that we shall have a perfect victory over satan and our enemies; and that God the Father hath given all power into the hands of Jesus Christ, who is our head and captain; that we may be partakers of it. Thus we see St. Paul's meaning. God hath witnessed, and we know it by experience, that he will never fail us in time of need. And why so? For he hath already saved us, in that he hath called us to the gospel, and redeemed us from sin. He hath called us with an holy calling; that is to say, he hath chosen us to himself, out of the general confusion of mankind.

The Lord having drawn us to him, will he not uphold us, and guide us to the end? This is a sure confirmation of the power of God; that we always find him ready to help us: therefore we put our trust in him, knowing that we have already felt his power. That we may profit by this doctrine, let us know first of all, that whereas God hath given us the knowledge of his truth, it is as much as if he had shown us already that we belonged to his heavenly inheritance, and that we were his, and of his flock. If we are persuaded of this, and resolved therein, we shall always go forward in the cause, knowing that we are under his protection. He hath sufficient strength to overcome all our enemies, which makes our salvation sure.

Let us not fear, on account of our weakness, for God hath promised to assist us. We should think upon this, and endeavour to receive that which is said to us. The Lord will bring our salvation to an end! He will assist us in the midst of pèrsecutions, and enable us to overcome them. When we are once convinced of these things, it will not require much power of rhetoric to strengthen us against temptations. We shall triumph over all our enemies: notwithstanding we seem to the world to be trodden under foot, and utterly overwhelmed. But we must come to this declaration which St. Paul addeth, concerning the salvation of which we have spoken, and the holy calling. He saith, "Not according to our works, but according to his own purpose and grace."

For he had no respect to our works or dignity, when he called us to salvation. He did it of mere grace. Therefore we shall be less excusable, if we disobey his requirements, seeing we have not only been purchased by the blood of our Lord Jesus Christ, but he had a care of our salvation before the world was made. Let us here observe that St. Paul condemneth our unthankfulness, if we be so unfaithful to God, as not to bear witness of his gospel; seeing he hath called us to it. And that he may better express this purpose, the apostle adds, that this "was given us in Christ Jesus before the world began;" before the world had its course, or beginning: it was revealed at the coming of our Lord Jesus Christ.

When this great Saviour made his appearance, the grace that was hid before, yea, and could not be reached by the knowledge of man, was made clear and manifest. And how so? The Son of God destroyed death, and also brought everlasting life! And we need not go afar off to find it, for the gospel leadeth us to it. When God sendeth us this message of salvation, we have only to receive the inheritance which he promised us. Let us open our mouths, that he may fill them; let us open our hearts, and give this testimony of the gospel leave to enter; and the immortality of the kingdom of heaven shall dwell within us; though we be poor, frail vessels, and have nothing but corruption and rottenness in us; yet notwithstanding, we do already lay hold upon this immortality, and have a sure witness of it, when we can accept this grace that is offered in the gospel.

That we may better understand what is here contained, let us remark that this word *purpose*, signifieth the everlasting decree of God; which hath no causes whatsoever. For when we speak of God's counsels, we need not dispute about who moved him: as though we should imagine reasons, and say, this is the reason why God hath determined after this sort; this is the cause why he would have it so. For God will have us use such soberness, that his bare will may suffice us for all reason. When it is said, God hath thus appointed it, though our eyes be dazzled, and the matter seem strange to us, and we see no reason why it should thus be, yet we must conclude that his will is just, of which we must not find fault. It is wisdom in us to do whatever God appointeth, and never ask why.

But because men have busy heads, and given much to curiosity, St. Paul bringeth us to God's purpose; and telleth us plainly, that we must consider it so deep that we cannot enter into it, to know who moved him. He was moved only by his just will; which is a rule of all justice. Therefore, we are hereby informed, that our salvation depends not upon our deserts: God never examined what we were, nor what we were worthy of, when he chose us to himself; but he had his purpose; that is, he sought no cause of our salvation but in himself. St.

Paul showeth evidently that this word *purpose*, signifieth this decree. But because men cannot by reason of the pride that is in them, withhold themselves from imagining some worthiness of their own, they think that God is under an obligation to seek them: but St. Paul saith pointedly, *purpose and grace*. This is as much as if he had said, free purpose.

This is therefore to beat down all our works: that we be not so foolish and stubborn, as to think God chose us because there was something in us worthy of it. No, no; but we must know that God never went farther than himself, when he chose us to salvation. For he saw that there was nothing but condemnation in us: therefore he contented himself, by mere grace and infinite mercy, to look upon our misery, and help us; although we were not worthy. For better proof hereof, St. Paul saith, that this grace was given us before the world began.

We perceive by this, how void of sense men are, when they vaunt themselves of believing that they are the cause of their own salvation; and have prevented God's goodness, or were before him, and met with him. Whereupon hangeth our salvation? Is it not upon the election and choice that hath been from everlasting? God chose us before we were. What could we do then? We were made fit, we were well disposed to come to God. Nay, we see that our salvation doth not begin after we have knowledge, discretion, and good desires; but it is grounded in God's everlasting decree, which was before any part of the world was made.

What can we do then? have we any means to put forth ourselves? can we give God occasion to call us, and separate us from the rest of the world? Are we not then marvellously mistaken, when we think we have some worthiness of our own, and exalt our deserts to darken God's grace, and be thus prepared of ourselves to have access to him? We must mark well for what purpose St. Paul here mentions the election of God ; saying, that grace was given us in Christ Jesus before the world began. They that think to abolish the doctrine of God's election, destroy as much as possible the salvation of the world.

This is the most fit instrument, used by the devil, to deface the virtue of the blood of our Lord Jesus Christ ; to bring to nought, and destroy the gospel ; yea, and to put the goodness of God out of man's memory. The devil hath no fitter instruments than those who fight against predestination ; and cannot in their rage suffer it to be spoken of, or preached as it ought to be. If we detest the *papists*, (as indeed they ought to be detested,) because they have profaned the holy scripture, and have marred and depraved the truth of the gospel and the service of God, by infecting all the world with superstition and idolatry, much more are they to be detested, who go about to bring to nought God's election ; and endeavour, by indirect and crooked ways, to stop men from speaking of it plainly and openly, and of preaching it as it ought to be.

Wherein consisteth the salvation of the faithful, only in God's free election ? Would we not have men preach that God hath chosen his, of mere goodness, without regard to any thing whatsoever ? Will we not admit this to be such a mystery as cannot be attained to ? showed and declared to us as far as God wished to reveal it ? If we do not admit this, we enter into a conspiracy with satan ; as though Jesus Christ suffered in vain, and the passion that he suffered, profited the world nothing. We may here remark, that the gospel cannot be preached, that it is a profane gospel, or the doctrine of Mahomet, that there is no church nor christianity, if God's election be abolished.

The Holy Ghost that speaketh here, must needs

be proved a liar, if this doctrine be not received. Therefore, let us fight constantly; for it is the groundwork of our salvation. How can we build, and maintain the building, if the foundation be destroyed? St. Paul showeth us here, with what virtue we must fight, and how we shall come to this inheritance, which was so dearly purchased for us: he showeth us how we shall enter into the possession of the glory of God, and make an end of this building and faith. My friends, we must be grounded upon the grace that was given us, not to-day nor yesterday, but before the world began.

It is true, God calleth us at this day, but his election goeth before; yea, and God chose us without any respect to our works, as we could have done nothing before: but we are debtors to him for all; for he drew us out of the bottomless pit of destruction, wherein we were cast, and past all hope of recovery. Therefore, there is good reason for us to submit ourselves wholly to him, and rely upon his goodness, and be thoroughly ravished with it. Let us hold fast this foundation, as I said before, unless we will have our salvation perish and come to nought. This doctrine is profitable for us, if we can apply it well to our own use.

They that would not have us speak of God's election, will say, it is not necessary. But such men never tasted God's goodness, neither do they know what it is to come to our Lord Jesus Christ. If we know not that we are saved because it pleased God to choose us before the world began, how can we know that which St. Paul saith to us; to wit, that we should give ourselves wholly to God, to be disposed of at his will, and to live and die in his service? How can we magnify his name? How can we confess that our salvation cometh from him only, that he is the beginning of it, and that we have not helped him therein? We may say it with our mouths, but unless we believe it, as it is here set forth, it will only be hypocrisy.

Therefore, let us learn that the doctrine of God's election, whereby we are taught that he predestinated us before the world began, ought to be preached openly and fully, in despite of all the world that would stand against it. And not only so, but we should know that it is a very profitable doctrine for us; because we cannot lay hold upon the infinite goodness of God, until we come thither. Unless this point be well cleared, God's mercy will be always disguised. I say, unless this be made plain to us, that he hath chosen us before we were born, and before we could prevent him.

Men will frequently say, that we were bought with the blood of our Lord Jesus Christ, and that we are not worthy that God should show us such great mercy: they will likewise say, who hath part and portion in such a redemption as God hath made in the person of his Son? Even they that will; they that seek God; even they that submit themselves to him. They that have some good motives, and are not rude; those that are good natured, and have some good devotion. When men make such a mixture, and think they are called to God, and to his grace, for something that is in themselves, that they bring something to recommend them to the favour of God, whereby they may attain salvation, the grace of God is darkened, and rent asunder.

This is a sacrilege that ought not to be countenanced. For this cause, I said the goodness of God shall never be thoroughly known, until this election be laid before us; and we are taught that we are called at this time, because it pleased God to extend his mercy to us before we were born. This doctrine must be explained more at large; but as time will not admit at present, we shall attend to it in the latter part of the day.

SERMON III.

2 Timothy, Chap. 1. *verses* 9 *and* 10.

9 Who hath saved us, and called us with an holy calling, not according to our works, but according to his own purpose and grace, which was given us in Christ Jesus before the world began;
10 But is now made manifest by the appearing of our Saviour Jesus Christ, who hath abolished death, and hath brought life and immortality to light through the gospel.

We have shown this morning, according to the text of St. Paul, that if we will know the free mercy of our God in saving us, we must come to his everlasting counsel : whereby he chose us before the world began. For there we see, he had no regard to our persons, neither to our worthiness, nor to any deserts that we could possibly bring. Before we were born, we were enrolled in his register; he had already adopted us for his children. Therefore let us yield the whole to his mercy, knowing that we cannot boast of ourselves, unless we rob him of the honour which belongs to him.

Men have endeavoured to invent cavils, to darken the grace of God. For they have said, although God chose men before the world began, yet it was according as he foresaw that one would be diverse from another. The scripture showeth plainly, that God did not wait to see whether men were worthy or not, when he chose them : but the sophisters thought they might darken the grace of God, by saying, though he regarded not the deserts that were passed, he had an eye to those that were to come. For, say they, though Jacob and his brother Esau had done neither good nor evil, and God chose one and refused the other, yet notwithstanding he foresaw, (as all things are present with him,) that Esau would be a vicious man, and that Jacob would be as he afterwards showed himself.

But these are foolish speculations: for they plainly make St. Paul a liar; who saith, God rendered no reward to our works when he chose us, because he did it before the world began. But though the authority of St. Paul were abolished, yet the matter is very plain and open, not only in the holy scripture, but in reason; insomuch that those who would make an escape after this sort, show themselves to be men void of all skill. For if we search ourselves to the bottom, what good can we find? Are not all mankind cursed? What do we bring from our mother's womb, except sin?

Therefore we differ not one whit, one from another; but it pleaseth God to take those to himself, whom he would. And for this cause, St. Paul useth these words in another place; when he saith, men have not whereof to rejoice, for no man finds himself better than his fellows, unless it be because God discerneth him. So then, if we confess that God chose us before the world began, it necessarily follows, that God prepared us to receive his grace; that he bestowed upon us that goodness, which was not in us before; that he not only chose us to be heirs of the kingdom of heaven, but he likewise justifies us, and governs us by his holy spirit. The christian ought to be so well resolved in this doctrine, that he is beyond doubt.

There are some men at this day, that would be glad if the truth of God were destroyed. Such men fight against the Holy Ghost, like mad beasts, and endeavour to abolish the holy scripture. There is more honesty in the papists, than in these men: for the doctrine of the papists is a great deal better, more holy, and more agreeable to the sacred scripture, than the doctrine of those vile and wicked men, who cast down God's holy election; these dogs that bark at it, and swine that root it up.

However, let us hold fast that which is here

taught us : God having chosen us before the world had its course, we must attribute the cause of our salvation to his free goodness ; we must confess that he did not take us to be his children, for any deserts of our own ; for we had nothing to recommend ourselves into his favour. Therefore, we must put the cause and fountain of our salvation in him only, and ground ourselves upon it : otherwise, whatsoever and howsoever we build, it will come to nought.

We must here notice what St. Paul joineth together ; to wit, the grace of Jesus Christ, with the everlasting counsel of God the Father : and then he bringeth us to our calling, that we may be assured of God's goodness, and of his will, that would have remained hid from us, unless we had a witness of it. St. Paul saith in the first place, that the grace which hangeth upon the purpose of God, and is comprehended in it, is given in our Lord Jesus Christ. As if he said, seeing we deserve to be cast away, and hated as God's mortal enemies, it was needful for us to be grafted, as it were, into Jesus Christ ; that God might acknowledge, and allow us for his children. Otherwise, God could not look upon us, only to hate us ; because there is nothing but wretchedness in us ; we are full of sin, and stuffed up as it were with all kinds of iniquity.

God, who is justice itself, can have no agreement with us, while he considereth our sinful nature. Therefore, when he would adopt us before the world began, it was requisite that Jesus Christ should stand between us and him ; that we should be chosen in his person, for he is the well beloved Son : when God joineth us to him, he maketh us such as pleaseth him. Let us learn to come directly to Jesus Christ, if we will not doubt God's election : for he is the true looking glass, wherein we must behold our adoption.

If Jesus Christ be taken from us, then is God a

judge of sinners; so that we cannot hope for any goodness or favour at his hands, but look rather for vengeance: for without Jesus Christ, his majesty will always be terrible and fearful to us. If we hear mention made of his everlasting purpose, we cannot but be afraid, as though he were already armed to plunge us into misery. But when we know that all grace resteth in Jesus Christ, then we may be assured that God loved us, although we were unworthy.

In the second place, we must notice that St. Paul speaketh not simply of God's election, for that would not put us beyond doubt; but we should rather remain in perplexity and anguish: but he adds, *the calling*; whereby God hath opened his counsel, which before was unknown to us, and which we could not reach. How shall we know then that God hath chosen us, that we may rejoice in him, and boast of the goodness that he hath bestowed upon us? They that speak against God's election, leave the gospel alone; they leave all that God layeth before us, to bring us to him; all the means that he hath appointed for us, and knoweth to be fit and proper for our use. We must not go on so; but according to St. Paul's rule, we must join the calling with God's everlasting election.

It is said, we are called; and thus we have this second word, calling. Therefore God calleth us: and how? Surely, when it pleaseth him to certify us of our election; which we could by no other means attain unto. For who can enter into God's counsel? as saith the prophet Isaiah; and also the apostle Paul. But when it pleaseth God to communicate himself to us familiarly, then we receive that which surmounteth the knowledge of all men: for we have a good and faithful witness, which is the Holy Ghost; that raiseth us above the world, and bringeth us even into the wonderful secrets of God.

We must not speak rashly of God's election, and

say, we are predestinate; but if we will be thoroughly assured of our salvation, we must not speak lightly of it; whether God hath taken us to be his children or not. What then? Let us look at what is set forth in the gospel. There God showeth us that he is our Father; and that he will bring us to the inheritance of life, having marked us with the seal of the Holy Ghost in our hearts, which is an undoubted witness of our salvation, if we receive it by faith.

The gospel is preached to a great number, which, notwithstanding, are reprobate; yea, and God discovereth and showeth that he hath cursed them: that they have no part nor portion in his kingdom, because they resist the gospel, and cast away the grace that is offered them. But when we receive the doctrine of God with obedience and faith, and rest ourselves upon his promises, and accept this offer that he maketh us, to take us for his children, this, I say, is a certainty of our election. But we must here remark, that when we have knowledge of our salvation, when God hath called us and enlightened us in the faith of his gospel, it is not to bring to nought the everlasting predestination that went before.

There are a great many in these days, that will say, who are they whom God hath chosen, but only the faithful? I grant it; but they make an evil consequence of it; and say, faith is the cause, yea, and the first cause of our salvation. If they called it a middle cause, it would indeed be true; for the scripture saith, Eph. ii. 8. "By grace are ye saved through faith." But we must go up higher; for if they attribute faith to men's free will, they blaspheme wickedly against God, and commit sacrilege. We must come to that which the scripture showeth; to wit, when God giveth us faith, we must know that we are not capable of receiving the gospel, only as he hath framed us by the Holy Ghost.

It is not enough for us to hear the voice of man, unless God work within, and speak to us in a secret manner by the Holy Ghost; and from hence cometh faith. But what is the cause of it? why is faith given to one and not to another? St. Luke showeth us: saying, Acts xiii. 48. "As many as were ordained to eternal life believed." There were a great number of hearers, and yet but few of them received the promise of salvation. And what few were they? Those that were appointed to salvation. Again, St. Paul speaketh so largely upon this subject, in his epistle to the Ephesians, that it cannot be but the enemies of God's predestination are stupid and ignorant, and that the devil hath plucked out their eyes; and that they have become void of all reason, if they cannot see a thing so plain and evident.

St. Paul saith, God hath called us, and made us partakers of his treasures and infinite riches, which were given us through our Lord Jesus Christ: according as he had chosen us before the world began. When we say that we are called to salvation because God hath given us faith, it is not because there is no higher cause; and whosoever cannot come to the everlasting election of God, taketh somewhat from him, and lesseneth his honour. This is found in almost every part of the holy scripture.

That we may make a short conclusion of this matter, let us see in what manner we ought to keep ourselves. When we inquire about our salvation, we must not begin to say, are we chosen? No, we can never climb so high; we shall be confounded a thousand times, and have our eyes dazzled, before we can come to God's counsel. What then shall we do? Let us hear what is said in the gospel: when God hath been so gracious, as to make us receive the promise offered, know we not that it is as much as if he had opened his whole heart to us, and had registered our election in our consciences!

We must be certified that God hath taken us for his children, and that the kingdom of heaven is ours; because we are called in Jesus Christ. How may we know this? How shall we stay ourselves upon the doctrine that God hath set before us? We must magnify the grace of God, and know that we can bring nothing to recommend ourselves to his favour; we must become nothing in our own eyes, that we may not claim any praise; but know that God hath called us to the gospel, having chosen us before the world began. This election of God is, as it were, a sealed letter; because it consisteth in itself, and in its own nature: but we may read it, for God giveth a witness of it, when he calleth us to himself by the gospel and by faith.

For even as the original or first copy taketh nothing from the letter or writing that is read, even so must we be out of doubt of our salvation. When God certifieth us by the gospel that he taketh us for his children, this testimony carries peace with it; being signed by the blood of our Lord Jesus Christ, and sealed by the Holy Ghost. When we have this witness, have we not enough to content our minds? Therefore, God's election is so far from being against this, that it confirmeth the witness which we have in the gospel. We must not doubt but what God hath registered our names before the world was made, among his chosen children: but the knowledge thereof he reserved to himself.

We must always come to our Lord Jesus Christ, when we talk of our election; for without him, (as we have already shown,) we cannot come nigh to God. When we talk of his decree, well may we be astonished, as men worthy of death. But if Jesus Christ be our guide, we may with cheerfulness depend upon him; knowing that he hath worthiness enough in him to make all his members beloved of God the Father; it being sufficient for us that we are grafted into his body, and made one with him. Thus we must muse upon this doctrine, if we will profit by it aright: as it is set forth by St. Paul; when he saith, this grace of salvation was given us *before the world began.* We must go beyond the order of nature, if we will know how we are saved, and by what cause, and from whence our salvation cometh.

God would not leave us in doubt, neither would he hide his counsel, that we might not know how our salvation was secured; but hath called us to him by his gospel, and hath sealed the witness of his goodness and fatherly love in our hearts. So then, having such a certainty, let us glorify God, that he hath called us of his free mercy. Let us rest ourselves upon our Lord Jesus Christ, knowing that he hath not deceived us, when he caused it to be preached, that he gave himself for us; and witnessed it by the Holy Ghost. For faith is an undoubted token that God taketh us for his children; and thereby we are led to the everlasting election, according as he had chosen us before.

He saith not that God hath chosen us because we have heard the gospel, but on the other hand, he attributes the faith that is given us to the highest cause; to wit, because God hath fore-ordained that he would save us; seeing we were lost and cast away in Adam. There are certain dolts, who, to blind the eyes of the simple, and such as are like themselves, say, the grace of salvation was given us, because God ordained that his Son should redeem mankind, and therefore this is common to all.

But St. Paul spake after another sort; and men cannot by such childish arguments mar the doctrine of the gospel: for it is said plainly, that God hath saved us. Does this refer to all without exception?

No; he speaketh only of the faithful. Again, does St. Paul include all the world? Some were called by preaching, and yet they made themselves unworthy of the salvation which was offered them: therefore they were reprobate. God left others in their unbelief, who never heard the gospel preached.

Therefore St. Paul directeth himself plainly and precisely to those whom God had chosen and reserved to himself. God's goodness will never be viewed in its true light, nor honoured as it deserveth, unless we know that he would not have us remain in the general destruction of mankind; wherein he hath left those that were like unto us: from whom we do not differ; for we are no better than they: but so it pleased God. Therefore all mouths must be stopped; men must presume to take nothing upon themselves, except to praise God, confessing themselves debtors to him for all their salvation.

We shall now make some remarks upon the other words used by St. Paul in this place. It is true that God's election could never be profitable to us, neither could it come to us, unless we knew it by means of the gospel; for this cause it pleased God to reveal that which he had kept secret before all ages. But to declare his meaning more plainly, he adds, that this grace is revealed to us now. And how? "By the appearing of our Saviour Jesus Christ." When he saith that this grace is revealed to us by the appearing of Jesus Christ, he showeth that we should be too unthankful, if we could not content and rest ourselves upon the grace of the Son of God. What can we look for more? If we could climb up beyond the clouds, and search out the secrets of God, what would be the result of it? Would it not be to ascertain that we are his children and heirs?

Now we know these things, for they are clearly set forth in Jesus Christ. For it is said, that all who believe in him, shall enjoy the privilege of being

God's children. Therefore we must not swerve from these things one jot, if we will be certified of our election. St. Paul hath already shown us, that God never loved us, nor chose us, only in the person of his beloved son. When Jesus Christ appeared, he revealed life to us; otherwise we should never have been the partakers of it. He hath made us acquainted with the everlasting counsel of God. But it is presumption for men, to attempt to know more than God would have them know.

If we walk soberly and reverently in obedience to God, hearing and receiving what he saith in the holy scripture, the way will be made plain before us. St. Paul saith, when the Son of God appeared in the world, he opened our eyes, that we might know that he was gracious to us before the world was made. We were received as his children, and accounted just; so that we need not doubt but that the kingdom of heaven is prepared for us. Not that we have it by our deserts, but because it belongs to Jesus Christ, who makes us partakers with himself.

When St. Paul speaketh of the appearing of Jesus Christ, he saith, "He hath brought life and immortality to light through the gospel." It is not only said that Jesus Christ is our Saviour, but that he is sent to be a mediator; to reconcile us by the sacrifice of his death: he is sent to us as a lamb without blemish; to purge us, and make satisfaction for all our trespasses: he is our pledge, to deliver us from the condemnation of death: he is our righteousness; he is our advocate, who maketh intercession with God, that he would hear our prayers.

We must allow all these qualities to belong to Jesus Christ, if we will know aright how he appeared. We must look at the substance contained in the gospel. We must know that Jesus Christ appeared as our Saviour, and that he suffered for our salvation; and that we were reconciled to God the

Father through his means; that we have been cleansed from all our blemishes, and freed from everlasting death. If we know not that he is our advocate, that he heareth us when we pray to God, to the end that our prayers may be answered, what will become of us? what confidence can we have to call upon God's name, who is the fountain of our salvation? But St. Paul saith, Jesus Christ hath fulfilled all things that were requisite for the redemption of mankind.

If the gospel were taken away, of what advantage would it be to us that the Son of God had suffered death, and risen again the third day for our justification? All this would be unprofitable to us. So then, the gospel putteth us in possession of the benefits that Jesus Christ hath purchased for us. And therefore, though he be absent from us in body, and is not conversant with us here on earth, it is not that he hath withdrawn himself, as though we could not find him; for the sun that shineth doth no more enlighten the world, than Jesus Christ showeth himself openly to those that have the eyes of faith to look upon him, when the gospel is preached. Therefore St. Paul saith, Jesus Christ hath brought *life to light*, yea, everlasting life.

He saith, the Son of God hath abolished death. And how did he abolish it? If he had not offered an everlasting sacrifice to appease the wrath of God, if he had not entered even to the bottomless pit to draw us from thence, if he had not taken our curse upon himself, if he had not taken away the burden wherewith we were crushed down, where should we have been? would death have been destroyed? Nay, sin would reign in us, and death likewise. And indeed, let every one examine himself, and we shall find that we are slaves to satan, who is the prince of death. So that we are shut up in this miserable slavery, unless God destroy the devil, sin, and death.

And this is done: but how? He hath taken away our sins by the blood of our Lord Jesus Christ.

Therefore, though we be poor sinners, and in danger of God's judgement, yet sin cannot hurt us; the sting, which is venomous, is so blunted that it cannot wound us, because Jesus Christ has gained the victory over it. He suffered not the shedding of his blood in vain; but it was a washing wherewith we were washed through the Holy Ghost; as is shown by St. Peter. And thus we see plainly, that when St. Paul speaketh of the gospel, wherein Jesus Christ appeared, and appeareth daily to us, he forgetteth not his death and passion, nor the things that pertain to the salvation of mankind.

We may be certified, that in the person of our Lord Jesus Christ, we have all that we can desire; we have full and perfect trust in the goodness of God, and the love he beareth us. But we see that our sins separate us from God, and cause a warfare in our members; yet we have an atonement through our Lord Jesus Christ. And why so? Because he hath shed his blood to wash away our sins; he hath offered a sacrifice whereby God hath become reconciled to us; to be short, he hath taken away the curse, that we may be blessed of God. Moreover, he hath conquered death, and triumphed over it; that he might deliver us from the tyranny thereof; which otherwise would entirely overwhelm us.

Thus we see, that all things that belong to our salvation, are accomplished in our Lord Jesus Christ. And that we may enter into full possession of all these benefits, we must know that he appeareth to us daily by his gospel. Although he dwelleth in his heavenly glory, if we open the eyes of our faith, we shall behold him. We must learn not to separate that which the Holy Ghost hath joined together. Let us observe what St. Paul meant by a comparison to amplify the grace that God showed to the world after the coming of our Lord Jesus Christ; as if he said, the old fathers had not this advantage; to have Jesus Christ appear to them, as he appeared to us.

It is true, they had the self-same faith; and the inheritance of heaven is theirs, as well as ours; God having revealed his grace to them as well as us: but not in like measure: for they saw Jesus Christ afar off, under the figures of the law, as St. Paul saith to the Corinthians. The veil of the temple was as yet stretched out, that the Jews could not come near the sanctuary: that is, the material sanctuary. But now, the veil of the temple being removed, we draw nigh to the majesty of our God: we come most familiarly to him, in whom dwelleth all perfection and glory. In short, we have the body, whereas they had but the shadow. Col. ii. 17.

The ancient fathers submitted themselves wholly to bear the affliction of Jesus Christ; as it is said in the 11th chapter of the Hebrews: for it is not said, Moses bore the shame of Abraham, but of Jesus Christ. Thus the ancient fathers, though they lived under the law, offered themselves to God in sacrifices, to bear most patiently the afflictions of Christ. And now, Jesus Christ having risen from the dead, hath brought *life to light*. If we are so delicate, that we cannot bear the afflictions of the gospel, are we not worthy to be blotted from the book of God, and cast off? Therefore, we must be constant in the faith, and ready to suffer for the name of Jesus Christ, whatsoever God will; because life is set before us, and we have a more familiar knowledge of it, than the ancient fathers had.

We know how the ancient fathers were tormented by tyrants, and enemies of the truth, and how they suffered constantly. The condition of the church is not more grievous in these days, than it was then. For now hath Jesus Christ brought life and immortality to light through the gospel. As often as the grace of God is preached to us, it is as much as if the kingdom of heaven were opened to us; as if God reached out his hand, and certified us that life was nigh; and that he will make us partakers of his heavenly inheritance. But when we look to this life, which was purchased for us by our Lord Jesus Christ, we should not hesitate to forsake all that we have in this world, to come to the treasure above, which is in heaven.

Therefore, let us not be willingly blind; seeing Jesus Christ layeth daily before us the life and immortality here spoken of. When St. Paul speaketh of life, and addeth immortality, it is as much as if he said, we already enter into the kingdom of heaven by faith. Though we be as strangers here below, the life and grace of which we are made partakers through our Lord Jesus Christ, shall bring its fruit in convenient time; to wit, when he shall be sent of God the Father, to show us the effect of things that are daily preached, which were fulfilled in his person, when he was clad in humanity.

SERMON IV.

2 TIMOTHY, Chap. ii. *verses* 16, 17, *and* 18.

16 But shun profane and vain babblings; for they will increase unto more ungodliness.
17 And their word will eat as doth a canker: of whom is Hymeneus and Philetus;
18 Who concerning the truth have erred, saying that the resurrection is past already; and overthrow the faith of some.

WE have already shown that St. Paul hath, not without cause, diligently exhorted Timothy to follow the pure simplicity of the word of God, without disguising it. The doctrine which is set forth to us in

God's name, to be the food of our souls, will be corrupted by the devil, if in his power : when he cannot destroy it, he blendeth things with it, in order to bring it into contempt, and destroy our knowledge of the will of God. There are many at this day, who put themselves forward to teach : and what is the cause of it ? Ambition carrieth them away : they disguise the word of God : and thus satan goeth about to deprive us of the spiritual life.

But this he is not able to accomplish, unless by some means the doctrine of God be corrupted. St. Paul repeateth the exhortation ; that we must shun all unprofitable babbling, and stay ourselves upon plain teaching, which is forcible. He not only condemneth manifest errours, superstition, and lies, but he condemneth the disguising of the word of God: as when men invent subtleties, to cloy men's ears ; bringing no true nourishment to the soul, nor edification in faith, and the fear of God, to the hearers.

When St. Paul speaketh of vain babbling, he meaneth that which contenteth curious men ; as we see many that take great pleasure in vain questions, wherewith they seem to be ravished. They do not openly speak against the truth, but they despise it as a thing too common and base ; as a thing for children and fools ; as for them, they will know some higher and more profound matter. Thus they are at variance with that which would be profitable for them. Therefore, let us weigh well the words of St. Paul ; *vain babbling ;* as though he said, if there be nothing but fine rhetorick, and exquisite words, to gain him credit that speaketh, and to show that he is well learned, none of this should be received into the church ; all must be banished.

For God will have his people to be edified ; and he hath appointed his word for that purpose. Therefore, if we go not about the salvation of the people, that they may receive nourishment by the doctrine that is taught them, it is sacrilege : for we pervert the pure use of the word of God. This word *profane*, is set against that which is holy and dedicated to God. Whatsoever pertaineth to the magnifying of God, and increases our knowledge of his majesty, whereby we may worship him : whatsoever draweth us to the kingdom of heaven, or taketh our affections from the world, and leadeth us to Jesus Christ, that we may be grafted into his body, is called holy.

On the contrary, when we feel not the glory of God, when we feel not to submit ourselves to him, when we know not the riches of the kingdom of heaven, when we are not drawn into his service to live in pureness of conscience, when we know not what the salvation meaneth which was purchased by our Lord Jesus Christ, we belong to the world, and are *profaned*. The doctrine which serves to mislead us in such things, is also called *profane*. Thus we see what St. Paul's meaning is : to wit, when we come together in the name of God, it is not to hear merry songs, and to be fed with wind ; that is, with vain and unprofitable curiosity ; but to receive spiritual nourishment. For God will have nothing preached in his name, but that which will profit and edify the hearers ; nothing but that which containeth good matter.

But it is true, our nature is such, that we take great pleasure in novelty, and in speculations which seem to be subtle. Therefore, let us beware, and think as we ought ; that we may not profane God's holy word. Let us seek that which edifieth, and not abuse ourselves by receiving that which hath no substance in it. It is hard to withdraw men from such vanity, because they are inclined to participate in it : But St. Paul showeth, that there is nothing more miserable than such vain curiosity : " For they will increase unto more ungodliness." As if he had said, my friends, you know not at first sight what hurt cometh by these deceivers; who go about to gain credit and estimation among you, and with pleasant toys endeavour to please you: but believe me, they are satan's instruments; and such as in no wise serve God; but increase unto more wickedness: that is, if they are let alone, they will mar the christian religion; they will not leave one jot safe and sound. Therefore, see that you flee them as plagues; although at first sight, the poison which they bring be not perceived.

Every one of us should suspect himself, when we have to judge of this doctrine. And why so? Because, (as I said before,) we are all weak; our minds are altering and changing; and besides, we have a foolish desire that draweth to things which are unprofitable. And therefore let us beware that we do not satisfy our own desires. Although this doctrine may not seem bad to us at the first view, yet notwithstanding, if it has not a tendency to lead us to God, and strengthen us in his service, to confirm us in the faith and hope that is given us of everlasting life, it will deceive us in the end; and prove to be but a mixture which serveth no purpose, except to take away the good which we had received before.

To be short, those that have not this in view, to draw the world to God, and build up the kingdom of our Lord Jesus Christ, that he may rule among us, mar all. All the labour and pains they take, but increases their wickedness: and if they be suffered to go on in this way, a gate is set open to satan, whereby he may bring to nought whatsoever is of God: although this is not done at the first blow, yet we see the end is such. To express this the better, St. Paul adds, "Their word will eat as doth a canker"

The word "*eat*," mentioned here, is not commonly understood; it is what the chirurgeons call, *an eating sore*; and what is also called, *St. Anthony's fire:* that is to say, when there is such an inflammation in any part of the body, that the sore eateth not only the flesh and sinews, but the bones also; in short, it is a fire that devoureth all: the hand will cause the arm to be lost, and the foot the leg; unless at the beginning, the part that is affected be cut off: thus, the man is in danger of losing his members, unless there be fit remedies provided for it; in this case we should spare no pains, but cut off the part affected, that the rest be not utterly destroyed.

Thus we view it here spiritually: for St. Paul showeth us, that although we may have been well instructed in wholesome doctrine, all will be marred, if we give place to these unprofitable questions, and only endeavour to please the hearers, and feed their desires. Seeing we understand what St. Paul's meaning is, let us endeavour to put this exhortation into practice. When we see men go about, endeavouring to turn us aside from the true doctrine, let us shun them, and shut the gate against them. Unless we take it in hand at the first start, and entirely cut it off, it may be as difficult to control, as the disease of which we have spoken.

Therefore, let us not be sleeping; for this is a matter of importance; it will prove a deadly disease, unless it be seen to in time. If this exhortation had been observed, things would be in a better condition at the present day in christendom. For this doltishness of papistry, is but the vain babbling spoken of by St. Paul. Even those who would be counted the greatest doctors among them, who are of many years standing, yea, and have spent their whole life in it, think upon nothing but foolish prat tling; which serveth no other purpose than to lead men astray: as no man knoweth what they mean. It seemeth that the devil hath forged this language by a miraculous subtlety, in order that he might bring all doctrine into confusion.

It is plainly perceived that they have conspired to do contrary to that which St. Paul hath in God's name forbidden. For they that have thus turned the word of God into a profane language of barbarous and unknown words, shall be much less able to excuse themselves. Many there are that would gladly have pleasant things taught them; they would make pastime of the word of God, and recreate themselves thereby; thus they seek vain and unprofitable teaching. They would bring errour, contention, and debate into the church, and endeavour to bring the religion we hold into doubt, and obscure the word of God.

Therefore we must be so much the more earnest to serve God, and continue constantly in the pureness of the gospel. If we have a desire to obey our God as we ought, we must practise that which is commanded us, and pray him to cleanse the church from these plagues; for they are the devil's instruments. This might be applied to all corruptions and stumbling-blocks invented by the devil; but it is here spoken of, concerning the doctrine whereby we are quickened; which is the true food of the soul.

Now let us come to that part of the subject, in which St. Paul informs us, who are of this number. He saith, "Of whom is Hymeneus, and Philetus; who concerning the truth have erred, saying that the resurrection is past already; and overthrow the faith of some." When he nameth Hymeneus and Philetus, he showeth that we must not spare them, who, like scabby sheep, may infect the flock: but we must rather tell every one, what kind of men they are ; that they may beware of them. Are we not traitors to our neighbours, when we see them in danger of being turned from God, and do not inform them of it ? A wicked man that goeth about to establish perverse doctrine, and cause offences in the church, what is he but an impostor ? If I dissemble when I see him, is it not as though I should see my neighbour in danger, and would not bid him beware ?

If the life of the body ought to be so precious to us, that we would do all in our power to preserve it, of how much more importance is the life of the soul ! Those who endeavour to turn every thing upside down, will come and sow their false doctrine among the people, in order to draw them into a contempt of God. These barking dogs, these vile goats, these ravenous wolves, are they that have erred, and endeavoured to overthrow the faith of the church : and yet we suffer them. Men will frequently say, must we be at defiance with them ? Must we cast them off, that they may fall into despair? This is said by those who think we ought to use gentleness ; but what mercy is it to spare one man, and in the mean time to cast away a thousand souls, rather than warn them ? We must not suffer wicked herbs to grow among us, lest they should get the upper hand, and choke whatsoever good seed there be, or utterly destroy it.

Satan cometh with his poison and plagues, that he may destroy all. We see the flock of God troubled and tormented with ravenous wolves, that devour and destroy whatsoever they can. Must we be moved with mercy towards a wolf ; and in the mean time let the poor sheep and lambs of which our Lord hath such a special care, let them, I say, perish ? When we see any wicked man troubling the church, either by offences or false doctrine, we must prevent him as much as lieth in our power: we must warn the simple, that they be not misled and carried away; this I say, is our duty.

The Lord would have the wicked made known, that the world may discern them, that their ungodliness may be made manifest to all. St. Paul speaketh of some, who are busy bodies, idlers, &c.: these must be pointed out likewise, that they may be shunned. What must be done to those who have the sword in hand; who have become very devils; who can in no wise live in peace and concord, but thrust themselves forward to bring all to nought? When we see them thus, must we hold our peace? Let us learn to know them that trouble the church of God, and keep them back, and endeavour to prevent them from doing injury. Hereby we see how few there are that have a zeal for God's church.

We speak not only of open enemies, (for we confess that we must name the *papists*, that we be not entangled with their errour and superstition,) but we see others that seek to turn us away from the simplicity of the gospel: they endeavour to bring all things into disorder; they sow tares, that they may bring this doctrine into hatred, and cause men to be grieved with it: others would have a licentious liberty, to do what wickedness they choose, and thus throw off the yoke of our Lord Jesus Christ. We see others, who seek nothing but to fill the world with wickedness, blasphemies, and vileness; and thus endeavour to tread the reverence of God under foot. We likewise see gross drunkards and tiplers, who endeavour to bring all men into confusion.

And yet, who is there among us that setteth himself against these things? Who is there that saith, let us beware and be watchful? On the contrary, those that ought to reprove such wickedness sharply, not only wink at it, and let it pass, but they favour it, and give it their support. We see the wickedness that overspreads the land ; we see those that endeavour to pervert and bring to nought our salvation, and bring the church of God into doubt : and shall we dissemble, and make as though we saw none of these things ? We may boast as much as we please about being christians, yet there are more devils among us than christians, if we countenance such things.

Therefore, let us look well to the doctrine which is here given us ; and if we see wicked persons trying to infect the church of God, to darken good doctrine, or destroy it, let us endeavour to bring their works to light, that every one may behold them : and thereby be enabled to shun them. If we attend not to these things, we are traitors to God, and have no zeal for his honour, nor for the salvation of the church. We must be professed enemies of wickedness, if we will serve God. It is not enough for us merely to refrain from committing sin, but we must condemn it as much as possible, that it may now bear any sway, or get the upper hand of us.

After St. Paul hath named these two individuals, he informs us, that they turned away from the faith, in somuch that they said the resurrection was passed. So we see their fall was horrible. Hymeneus and Philetus were not obscure men ; for St. Paul makes mention of them, although they were afar off; Timothy being at this time in Ephesus : it is therefore evident that they were famous men. They had been for some time in great reputation, as chief pillars in the church. But we see how far they fell ; even to renounce everlasting salvation which was purchased for us by our Lord Jesus Christ. If we look not for the resurrection, of what use is it for us to teach that there is a redeemer who hath saved us from the slavery of death ? Of what use will the death and passion of our Lord Jesus Christ be to us, unless we wait for the fruit that is promised us in the latter day, at his coming?

Notwithstanding these men had been for a season of the number of the faithful, yet they fell, as it were, into the bottomless gulf of hell. Thus God declareth his vengeance toward them that abuse his gospel. It seemeth that these men were drunken with foolish ambition: they sought nothing but renown; they disguised the simplicity of the word of God, and endeavoured to show themselves greater than others. But God esteemeth his word far higher than he doth man; for if men cast it down and make a mock of it, he will not hold them guiltless. Thus we see that those who were like angels, have become very devils: they are blinded, and yet they would become great doctors.

The ability of these persons, of whom St. Paul speaketh, were not of the common sort; they were not idiots, but of high standing in all the churches: and yet they are fallen into such blindness, that they deny the resurrection of the dead: that is, they renounce the chiefest article of our religion, and deprive themselves of all hope of salvation. How is this possible! It seemeth strange that men who were able to teach others, should come to such gross and beastly ignorance. Thus we see how God revengeth scoffers and scorners that abuse his word. It cannot be but he must cast them off, into a state of reprobation; that they may never be able to discern any more, and become utterly void of all reason.

Therefore, if at this day, we see men become beastly, after having known the truth of God, and become void of reason, we must know that God will thereby magnify his word, and cause us to feel the majesty thereof. And why so? Because he punisheth the contempt of it, by giving such persons to the devil; and giving him full liberty over them. Therefore we must not be offended, when we see those who have tasted the gospel, revolt from the obedience of God; but let it rather be a confirmation of our faith: for God showeth us plainly that his word is of such importance, that he cannot in any wise have men abuse it, nor take it in vain; neither disguise or profane it.

We must learn to take heed, and walk fearfully and carefully. Let us view these things as a looking-glass set before our eyes, that we may see those who seemed to be passing for good christians, fallen; having in themselves nothing but wickedness, using detestable speeches, having nothing but filthiness in all their lives. Seeing God hath placed these things before us, let us take warning thereby, and awake and walk in the simplicity of the gospel, that we may not become a prey to satan.

It is true, these men had a fantastical resurrection as some do at the present day; who would make us believe, that to become christians, was to rise again: but the scripture calleth us to the coming of our Lord Jesus Christ, that we be always ready and prepared, that he may be made manifest; and until that time our life is hidden, and we are, as it were, in the shadow of death. When the scripture calleth us to our Lord Jesus, these fanaticks say, we must look for no other resurrection, except that which takes place when we are enlightened in the gospel.

We will here observe, that our old man must be crucified, if we will be partakers of the glory of our Lord Jesus Christ, and rise again with him. St. Paul hath shown us, that if we will be of the kingdom of our Lord Jesus Christ, we must be partakers of his cross; we must walk in death before we can come to life. How long will this death continue? As long as we are in this world. Therefore St. Peter saith, baptism is, as it were, a figure of the ark of Noah. 1 Pet. iii. 21. For we must be enclosed, as it were, in a grave; being dead to the world, if we will be quickened by the mark of our Lord Jesus Christ.

They that would have a resurrection at midway, do they not pervert the nature of baptism, and consequently all the order that God hath set among us? Let us learn, that until God shall take us out of this world, we must be as pilgrims in a strange country: and that our salvation shall not be shown us, until the coming of our Lord Jesus Christ: for he has become the first fruits of them that slept. 1 Cor. xv. And likewise, "He is the head of the body, the church; who is the beginning, the first-born from the dead; that in all things he might have the preeminence." Col. i. 18. It is true that Jesus Christ has risen again; but he must needs appear to us, and his life and glory must be shown us, before we can come to him.

St. John saith, that we are sure we are God's children: that we shall see him even as he is, when we shall be made like him. It is true, God is revealed to us when he transformeth us into his image; but that which we conceive by faith, is not yet seen, we must hope for it at the coming of our Lord Jesus Christ. Notwithstanding the great absurdity of the errour, St. Paul informs us that the two individuals here spoken of, have overthrown the faith of some. This is a thing that ought to make us tremble; to think that a doctrine which ought to be laid aside at the first sight, should overthrow the faith of some.

We see how the children of God are afflicted in this world; yea, it is often pitiable to behold their situation; while the unbelievers who contemn God, are at their ease, and live in pleasure: they make their triumph: whereas the saints are made as the off-scouring of the world. 1 Cor. iv. 13. How is it possible for men to conceive this heresy; to say the resurrection is already past ? And yet we see that this was welcome to some ; yea, in the primitive church ; in the time of the apostles. When they, whom Jesus Christ had chosen to preach his truth throughout the world, still lived, some fell from the faith.

When we see such an example, have we not occasion to be astonished, and walk in fear ! Not that we should doubt but what God will help and guide us, but it behooveth us to arm ourselves with prayer, and rely upon the promises of our God. Well may we be amazed, when we think upon the heinousness of this errour ; that God hath suffered some to be turned away from the faith already. If the apostles, who exercised all the power that was given them from above, to maintain the truth of God, could not prevent men from being misled, what must we expect now-a-days ! Let us be diligent in prayer, and flee to God that he may preserve us by his holy spirit. May we not be puffed up with presumption, but consider our nothingness ; for we should quickly be overthrown, if we were not upheld by the supreme Being.

These lessons are not given us without a cause. Although Hymeneus and Philetus are not alive at this day, yet in their persons the Holy Ghost meant to degrade the wicked, who go about to pervert our faith ; that we may not be grieved at whatsoever comes to pass ; that we may not depart from the good way, but be guarded against all offences. We must not be so puffed up with pride, as to go astray after our own foolish imaginations ; but we must take heed, and keep ourselves in obedience to the word of God : then we shall be daily more and more confirmed, until our good God taketh us to his everlasting rest, whereunto we are called.

SERMON V.

Titus, Chap. i. *verses* 15 *and* 16.

15 Unto the pure all things are pure; but unto them that are defiled and unbelieving is nothing pure; but even their mind and conscience is defiled.
16 They profess that they know God; but in works they deny him: being abominable and disobedient, and unto every good work reprobate.

St. Paul hath shown us that we must be ruled by the word of God; and hold the commandments of men as vain and foolish; for holiness and perfection of life belongeth not to them. He condemneth some of their commandments; as when they forbid certain meats, and will not suffer us to use that liberty which God giveth the faithful. Those who troubled the church in St. Paul's time, by setting forth such traditions, used the commandments of the law as a shield. These were but men's inventions: because the temple was to be abolished at the coming of our Lord Jesus Christ. Those in the church of Christ, who hold this superstition, to have certain meats forbidden, have not the authority of God, for it was against his mind and purpose that the christian should be subject to such ceremonies.

To be short, St. Paul informs us in this place, that in these days we have liberty to eat of all kinds of meat without exception. As for the health of the body, that is not here spoken of; but the matter here set forth is, that men shall not set themselves up as masters, to make laws for us contrary to the word of God. Seeing it is so, that God putteth no difference between meats, let us so use them; and never inquire what men like, or what they think good. Notwithstanding, we must use the benefits that God hath granted us, soberly and moderately. We must remember that God hath made meats for us, not that we should fill ourselves like swine, but that we should use them for the sustenance of life : therefore, let us content ourselves with this measure, which God hath shown us by his word.

If we have not such a store of nourishment as we would wish, let us bear our poverty patiently, and practise the doctrine of St. Paul; and know as well how to bear poverty, as riches. If our Lord give us more than we could have wished for, yet must we bridle our appetites. On the other side, if it please him to cut off our morsel, and feed us but poorly, we must be content with it; and pray him to give us patience when we have not what our appetites crave. To be short, we must have recourse to what is said in Romans xiii. "But put ye on the Lord Jesus Christ, and make not provision for the flesh, to fulfil the lusts thereof." Let us content ourselves to have what we need, and that which God knoweth to be proper for us; thus shall all things be clean to us, if we be thus cleansed.

Yet it is true, that although we were ever so unclean, the meats which God hath made are good; but the matter we have to consider, is the use of them. When St. Paul saith, *all things are clean*, he meaneth not that they are so of themselves, but as relateth to those that receive them; as we have noticed before; where he saith to Timothy, all things are sanctified to us by faith and giving of thanks. God hath filled the world with such abundance, that we may marvel to see what a fatherly care he hath over us : for to what end or purpose are all the riches here on earth, only to show how liberal he is toward man !

If we know not that he is our Father, and acteth the part of a nurse toward us ; if we receive not at his hand that which he giveth us, insomuch that when we eat, we are convinced that it is God that nourisheth us, he cannot be glorified as he deserveth: neither can we eat one morsel of bread without committing sacrilege; for which we must give an account. That we may lawfully enjoy these benefits, which have been bestowed upon us, we must be resolved upon this point, (as I said before,) that it is God that nourisheth and feedeth us.

This is the cleanness spoken of here by the apostle; when he saith, all things are clean, especially when we have such an uprightness in us, that we despise not the benefits bestowed upon another; but crave our daily bread at the hand of God, being persuaded that we have no right to it, only to receive it as the mercy of God. Now let us see from whence this cleanness cometh. We shall not find it in ourselves, for it is given us by faith. St. Peter saith, Acts xv. the hearts of the old fathers were cleansed by this means; to wit, when God gave them *faith.*

It is true that he here hath regard to the everlasting salvation; because we were utterly unclean until God made himself known to us in the name of our Lord Jesus Christ; who, being made our redeemer, brought the price and ransom of our souls. But this doctrine may, and ought to be applied to what concerneth this present life; for until we know, that being adopted in Jesus Christ, we are God's children, and consequently that the inheritance of this world is ours, if we touch one morsel of meat, we are thieves; for we are deprived of, and banished from all the blessings that God made, by reason of Adam's sin; until we get possession of them in our Lord Jesus Christ.

Therefore, it is faith that must cleanse us: then will all meats be clean to us: that is, we may use them freely without wavering. If men enjoin spiritual laws upon us, we need not observe them, being assured that such obedience cannot please God, for in so doing, we set up rulers to govern us, making them equal with God, who reserveth all power to himself. Thus, the government of the soul must be kept safe and sound in the hands of God. Therefore, if we allow so much superiority to men, that we suffer them to inwrap our souls with their own bands, we so much lessen and diminish the power and empire that God hath over us.

And thus, the humbleness that we might have in obeying the traditions of men, would be worse than all the rebellion in the world; because it is robbing God of his honour, and giving it, as a spoil, to mortal men. St. Paul speaketh of the superstition of some of the Jews, who would have men still observe the shadows and figures of the law; but the Holy Ghost hath pronounced a sentence, which must be observed to the end of the world; that God hath not bound us at this day to such a burden as was borne by the old fathers; but hath cut off that part which he had commanded, relative to the abstaining from meats; for it was a law but for a season.

Seeing God hath thus set us at liberty, what rashness it is for worms of the earth to make new laws; as though God had not been wise enough. When we allege this to the papists, they answer, that St. Paul spake of the Jews, and of meats that were forbidden by the law: this is true; but let us see whether this answer be to any purpose, or worth receiving. St. Paul not only saith, that it is lawful for us to use that which was forbidden, but he speaketh in general terms; saying, *all things are clean.* Thus we see that God hath here given us liberty, concerning the use of meats; so that he will not hold us in subjection, as were the old fathers.

Therefore, seeing God hath abrogated that law which was made by him, and will not have it in force any longer, what shall we think when we see men inventing traditions of their own; and not content themselves with what God hath shown them? In the first place, they still endeavour to hold the church of Christ under the restrictions of the old testament,

But God will have us governed as men of years and discretion, which have no need of instruction suitable for children. They set up man's devices, and say we must keep them under pain of deadly sin: whereas, God will not have his own law to be observed among us at this day, relative to types and shadows, because it was all ended at the coming of our Lord Jesus Christ.

Shall it then be lawful to observe what men have framed in their own wisdom? Do we not see that it is a matter which goeth directly against God? St. Paul setteth himself against such deceivers: against such as would bind christians to abstain from meats; as God had commanded in his law. If a man say, it is but a small matter to abstain from flesh on Friday, or in Lent, let us consider whether it be a small matter to corrupt and bastardize the service of God! For surely those that go about to set forth, and establish the tradition of men, set themselves against that which God hath appointed in his word; and thus commit sacrilege.

Seeing God will be served with obedience, let us beware and keep ourselves within those bounds which God hath set; and not suffer men to add any thing to it of their own. There is something worse in it than all this: for they think it a service that deserveth something from God, to abstain from eating flesh. They think it a great holiness: and thus the service of God, which should be spiritual, is banished, as it were, while men busy themselves about foolish trifles. As the common saying is, they leave the apple for the paring.

We must be faithful, and stand fast in our liberty; we must follow the rule which is given us in the word of God, and not suffer our souls to be brought into slavery by new laws, forged by men. For it is a hellish tyranny, which lesseneth God's authority, and mixeth the truth of the gospel with the figures of the law ; and perverteth and corrupteth the true service of God, which ought to be spiritual. Therefore, let us consider how precious a privilege it is to give thanks to God with quietness of conscience, being assured it is his will and pleasure that we should enjoy his blessings: and that we may do so, let us not entangle ourselves with the superstitions of men, but be content with what is contained in the pure simplicity of the gospel. Then, as we have shown concerning the first part of our text, *unto them that are pure, all things will be pure.*

When we have received the Lord Jesus Christ, we know that we shall be cleansed from our filthiness and blemishes ; for by his grace, we are made partakers of God's benefits, and are taken for his children, although there be nothing but vanity in us. "But unto them that are defiled and unbelieving, is nothing pure." By this St. Paul meaneth, that whatsoever proceedeth from those that are defiled and unbelieving, is not acceptable to God ; but is full of infection. While they are unbelieving, they are foul and unclean ; and while they have such filthiness in them, whatsoever they touch, becomes polluted with their infamy.

Therefore, all the rules and laws they can make, shall be nothing but vanity : for God disliketh whatsoever they do ; yea, he utterly abhorreth it. Although men may torment themselves with ceremonies and outward performances, yet all these things are vain, until they become upright in heart: for in this the true service of God commenceth. So long then as we are faithless, we are filthy before God. These things ought to be evident to us ; but hypocrisy is so rooted within us, that we are apt to neglect them. It will readily be confessed, that we cannot please God by serving him, until our hearts be rid of wickedness.

God strove with the people of old time about the same doctrine ; as we see, especially in the second chapter of the prophet Haggai: where he asketh the priests, if a man touch a holy thing, whether he shall be made holy or not; the priests answered, no. On the contrary, if an unclean man touch a thing, whether it shall become unclean or no: the priests answered and said, it shall be unclean: so is this nation, saith the Lord; and so are the works of their hands. Now let us notice what is contained in the figures and shadows of the law. If an unclean man had handled any thing, it became unclean; and therefore must be cleansed. Our Lord saith, consider what ye be: for ye have nothing but uncleanness and filth: yet notwithstanding, ye would content me with your sacrifices, offerings, and such like things. But he saith, as long as your minds are entangled with wicked lusts; as long as some of ye are whoremongers, adulterers, blasphemers, and perjurers; as long as ye are full of guile, cruelty, and spitefulness, your lives are utterly lawless, and full of all uncleanness; I cannot abide it, how fair soever it may seem before men.

We see then that all the services we can perform, until we are truly reformed in our hearts, are but mockeries; and God condemneth and rejecteth every whit of them. But who believeth these things to be so? When the wicked, who are taken in their wickedness, feel any remorse of conscience, they will endeavour by some means or other to compound with God, by performing some ceremonies: they think it sufficient to satisfy the minds of men, believing that God ought likewise to be satisfied therewith. This is a custom which has prevailed in all ages.

It is not only in this text of the prophet Haggai that God rebuketh men for their hypocrisy, and for thinking that they may obtain his favour with trifles, but it was a continual strife which all the prophets had with the Jews. It is said in Isa. i. 13, 14, 15. Bring no more vain oblations; incense is an abomination unto me; the new-moons and sabbaths, the calling of assemblies, I cannot away with : it is iniquity, even the solemn meeting, your new-moons and your appointed feasts my soul hateth : they are a trouble unto me ; I am weary to bear them. And when ye spread forth your hands, I will hide mine eyes from you ; yea, when ye make many prayers, I will not hear : your hands are full of blood."

And again it is said, Amos v. 22. " Though ye offer me burnt-offerings, and your meat-offerings, I will not accept them ; neither will I regard the peace-offerings of your fat beasts." God here showeth us that the things which he himself had commanded, were filthy and unclean when they were observed and abused by hypocrites. Therefore, let us learn that when men serve God after their own fashion, they beguile and deceive themselves. It is said in another text of Isaiah, " Who hath required these things at your hands ?" Wherein it is made manifest, that if we will have God approve our works, they must be according to his divine word.

Thus we see what St. Paul's meaning is, when he saith there is nothing *clean* to them that are *unclean*. And why? *For even their mind and conscience are defiled.* By this he showeth, (as I before observed,) that until such times as we have learned to serve God aright, in a proper manner, we shall do no good at all by our own works ; although we may flatter ourselves that they are of great importance, and by this means rock ourselves to sleep.

Let us now see what the traditions of *popery* are. The chief end of them are, to make an agreement with God, by their works of supererogation, as they term them : that is, their surplus works ; which are, when they do more than God commandeth them. According to their own notions, they discharge their duty towards him, and content him with such payment as they render by their works, and thereof make their account. When they have fasted their *saints* evenings, when they have refrained from eating flesh upon Fridays, when they have attended mass devoutly, when they have taken holy water, they think that God ought not to demand any thing more of them; and that there is nothing amiss in them.

But in the mean time, they cease not to indulge themselves in lewdness, whoredom, perjury, blasphemy, &c.: every one of them giving himself to those vices; yet notwithstanding, they think God ought to hold himself well paid with the works they offer him; as for example, when they have taken holy water, worshipped images, rambled from altar to altar, and other like things, they imagine that they have made sufficient payment and recompense for their sins: but we hear the doctrine of the Holy Ghost concerning such as are defiled; which is, there is nothing pure nor clean in all their doings.

But we will put the case, by supposing that all the abominations of the papists were not evil in their own nature; yet notwithstanding, according to this doctrine of St. Paul, there can be nothing but uncleanness in them, for they themselves are sinful and unclean. The holiness of these men consists in gewgaws and trifles. They endeavour to serve God in the things that he doth not require, and at the same time leave undone things that he hath commanded in his law.

It has been the case in all ages, that men have despised God's law for the sake of their own traditions. Our Lord Jesus Christ upbraided the pharisees, when he saith, Mat. xv. 3. "Why do ye also transgress the commandment of God by your tradition." Thus it was in former times, in the days of the prophets. Isaiah crieth out, chap. xxix. 13. "Wherefore the Lord said, forasmuch as this people draw near me with their mouth, and with their lips do honour me, but have removed their heart far from me, and their fear toward me is taught by the precept of men: therefore, behold, I will proceed to do a marvellous work and wonder ; for the wisdom of their wise men shall perish, and the understanding of their prudent men shall be hid." While men occupy themselves about traditions, they pass over the things that God hath commanded in his word.

This it is that caused Isaiah to cry out against such as set forth men's traditions ; telling them plainly that God threatened to blind the wisest of them, because they turned away from the pure rule of his word to follow their own foolish inventions. St. Paul likewise alludes to the same thing, when he saith, they have no fear of God before their eyes. Let us not deceive ourselves ; for we know that God requireth men to live uprightly, and to abstain from all violence, cruelty, malice, and deceit ; that none of these things should appear in our life. But those that have no fear of God before their eyes, it is apparent that they are out of order, and that there is nothing but uncleanness in their whole life.

If we wish to know how our life should be regulated, let us examine the contents of the word of God ; for we cannot be sanctified by outward show and pomp, although they are so highly esteemed among men. We must call upon God in sincerity, and put our whole trust in him ; we must give up pride and presumption, and resort to him with true lowliness of mind : that we be not given to fleshly affections. We must endeavour to hold ourselves in awe, under subjection to God, and flee from gluttony, whoredom, excess, robbery, blasphemy, and other evils. Thus we see what God would have us do, in order to have our life well regulated.

When men would justify themselves by outward works, it is like covering a heap of filth with a clean linen cloth. Therefore, let us put away the filthiness that is hidden in our hearts ; I say, let us drive the evil from us, and then the Lord will accept of our life: thus we may see wherein consists the true knowledge of God! When we understand this aright, it will lead us to live in obedience to his will. Men have not become so beastly, as to have no understanding that there is a God, who created them. But this knowledge, if they do not submit to his requirements, serves as a condemnation to them: because their eyes are blindfolded by satan; insomuch, that although the gospel may be preached to them, they do not understand it; in this situation we see many at the present day. How many there are in the world, that have been taught by the doctrine of the gospel, and yet continue in brutish ignorance!

This happeneth, because satan hath so prepossessed the minds of men with wicked affections, that although the light may shine ever so bright, they still remain blind, and see nothing at all. Let us learn then, that the true knowledge of God is of such a nature, that it showeth itself, and yieldeth fruit through our whole life. Therefore to know God, as St. Paul said to the Corinthians, we must be transformed into his image. For if we pretend to know him, and in the mean time our life be loose and wicked, it needeth no witness to prove us liars; our own life beareth sufficient record that we are mockers and falsifiers, and that we abuse the name of God.

St. Paul saith in another place, if ye know Jesus Christ, ye must put off the old man: as if he should say, we cannot declare that we know Jesus Christ, only by acknowledging him for our head; and by his receiving us as his members; which cannot be done until we have cast off the old man, and become new creatures. The world hath at all times abused God's name wickedly, as it doth still at this day; therefore, let us have an eye to the true knowledge of the word of God, whereof St. Paul speaketh.

Finally, let us not put our own works into the balance, and say they are good, and that we think well of them; but let us understand that the good works are those which God hath commanded in his law; and that all we can do beside these, are nothing. Therefore, let us learn to shape our lives according to what God hath commanded: to put our trust in him, to call upon him, to give him thanks, to bear patiently whatsoever it pleaseth him to send us; to deal uprightly with our neighbours; and to live honestly before all men. These are the works which God requireth at our hands.

If we were not so perverse in our nature, there would be none of us but what might discern these things: even children would have skill enough to discern them. The works which God hath not commanded, are but foolishness and an abomination; whereby God's pure service is marred. If we wish to know what constitutes the good works spoken of by St. Paul, we must lay aside all the inventions of men, and simply follow the instructions contained in the word of God; for we have no other rule than that which is given by him; which is such as he will accept, when we yield up our accounts at the last day, when he alone shall be the judge of all mankind.

Now let us fall down before the face of our good God, acknowledging our faults, praying him to make us perceive them more clearly: and to give us such trust in the name of our Lord Jesus Christ, that we may come to him, and be assured of the forgiveness of our sins; and that he will make us partakers of sound faith, whereby all our filthiness may be washed way.

SERMON VI.

2 Timothy, Chap. ii. *verse* 19.

19 Nevertheless the foundation of God standeth sure, having this seal, The Lord knoweth them that are his. And, let every one that nameth the name of Christ depart from iniquity.

We noticed this morning what was said by St. Paul concerning those that had fallen away; in order to stir up the minds of the faithful, to the end they should not be troubled thereat. If we see those fall who seemed to uphold the church, as it were, we must not be shaken; for if men be frail, if they go astray out of the right way, if they be froward, it is no new thing, for such is their nature; therefore we ought not to marvel at it, if they fall into wickedness rather than godliness. But in the mean time, our salvation is settled upon the grace of our God; yea, insomuch that it pleased him to choose us before the world began, and to make us of the number of his chosen children.

But we are grieved to see those who have shown some good tokens that they were the children of God, turn back; for we ought to possess a zeal to have the church of God enlarged and increased, rather than diminished. We ought also to have a care of our brethren, and to be sorry to see them perish; for it is no small matter to have the souls perish, who were bought by the blood of Christ. Yet notwithstanding, we must always comfort ourselves with this doctrine, that God will maintain his church, although the number be but small; though it be not so great as we could wish it, yet we must content ourselves, and believe he will safely keep all those he hath chosen.

Those that fall away, and those backsliders that renounce Jesus Christ, although they were joined to us, we must conclude that they were not of this number ; seeing they have departed from us. For it is easier for the world to be turned about a thousand times, than that one of God's chosen children, whom he holdeth fast to himself, should perish : it cannot be ! For God is the protector of our salvation, as he himself hath declared : yea, and this office is given to our Lord Jesus Christ, to maintain and keep all that God the Father hath chosen. This is what St. Paul meaneth by these words, *The foundation of God standeth sure, having this seal, the Lord knoweth them that are his.*

St. Paul setteth down two articles, which we shall here notice. In the first place, when we see such turning, that those who seemed to be the forwardest in religion, give back, and fall away from us, and so estrange themselves from the kingdom of God that they become unbelievers, we must not think that the church falleth. It is true, the number of those whom we thought to be faithful, is lessened by this means. But howsoever the world go, there is a sure foundation ; that is to say, God will always keep his church, and there shall always be some to call upon him, and worship him ; therefore let this be sufficient for us. For he hath declared, Psalm lxxii. that so long as the sun and moon endure, he will have some people to fear him, throughout all generations.

If we see the devil scatter the flock of our Lord Jesus Christ, if we see those that have given some proof of a good hope fall away, yet notwithstanding, we may be assured that the building remaineth ; even though it be hid from our view ; for it hath remained when there was scarcely a christian to be found in all the world. In what case were we forty years ago, before God gave us the light of his gospel ? Would it not have been thought that all christianity had been banished out of the world ? But yet there was a foundation hid ; that is, God reserved after a wonderful manner, such as he would, though it were but a small number. Therefore, *the foundation of God standeth sure.*

When we see such troubles, that we think all will come to nought, let us behold by faith this *foundation,* which cannot be seen by the eye of man. For if we have not faith to discern the church of God, we shall think it utterly abolished. We see what came to pass in the days of the prophet Elijah: he saith, 1 Kings xix. 14. "The children of Israel have forsaken thy covenant, thrown down thine altars, and slain thy prophets with the sword; and I, even I only, am left; and they seek my life, to take it away." But the Lord reproveth him, by telling him that he hath yet seven thousand in Israel, who have not bowed the knee to Baal. And so it will be at all times and seasons; we may think the church of God is utterly defaced and abolished, but he will keep the foundation sure.

Secondly, St. Paul informs us, that although the foundation of God standeth sure, yet it is as a letter closed up and sealed. And why so? Because *the Lord knoweth them that are his.* If God humble us, and blind us as it were, we must be content therewith; for he hath made his election sure, though it be hid from us. Although he will not make it known at first, yet notwithstanding, it remaineth in his secret counsel. Therefore if God know them that are his, let us not think it strange if we be often deceived when men revolt. Why so? For we know them not; but God will not be deceived; he will bring to an end whatsoever he hath determined in the counsel of his own will.

St. Paul exhorteth us not to be negligent, when we see those that were like angels among us fall from the right way: but to walk in fear and trembling; and beware that we do not abuse the name of God, by cloaking ourselves falsely with the name of christianity, as do the hypocrites; who take the name of God in their mouth, and at the same time mock him, and falsify his holy precepts. Let us practise that which is here contained; to wit, that if we call upon the name of our Lord Jesus Christ, if we make profession to be his, we must *depart from iniquity.* For we are not of the church of God, unless we separate ourselves from the world, and from the subtleties thereof.

Therefore, let us consider whereunto we are called; what our condition is: and then let us be faithful, and walk uprightly: for God can easily cut us off from his church, seeing he hath shown us such examples, if we have not made our profit by them.

But now, that we may apply this text better to our instruction, let us treat upon the point we have already mentioned; namely, the everlasting counsel of God, whereupon our election is grounded; upon which our salvation is surely settled. It is true, (as the scripture saith,) that we are saved by faith; for we know not that God is our Father, and that we are made partakers with him, only by faith, and by laying hold of the promises contained in the gospel; wherein God showeth that he accepteth us, and is pleased with us, in the name of our Lord Jesus Christ.

We must accept of this benefit, or we cannot know him. So then, we are in possession of our salvation by faith. This is true; but who is it that giveth us faith, save God alone? And why doth he give it to us? Because it pleased him to choose us before we were made; yea, before the world itself was made; as St. Paul showeth, especially in the first chapter to the Ephesians. He setteth that before us, which is most familiar to us; even that which we know; to wit, that God hath made us partakers of his heavenly blessings through Jesus Christ: that after he hath forgiven us our sins, he showeth us that we are acceptable to him, and that he hath taken us to be his children. Thus we have all that the gospel openeth to us.

But St. Paul lifteth us up higher; saying, all that is given us, is because God had chosen us before the world began; because he loved us in our Lord Jesus Christ before we could do either good or evil. This is what we shall now notice: namely; although God draweth us to him by the gospel, and we by faith receive the righteousness of our Lord Jesus Christ, who is the cause of our salvation; yet notwithstanding, there was a secret love of God that went before: yea, though it were hid from us, though God made no great haste in drawing us to him, yet it is certain that we were chosen. This is what St. Paul aimeth at in the sentence before us; to wit, *The foundation of God standeth sure.*

He setteth this foundation of God, against whatsoever virtue may be found in man: he setteth this sureness of which he speaketh, against this frail state of ours. St. Paul, knowing that we are inconstant, and that we straightway fall and pass away like water, saith, we must take our sureness in God; for we perceive it is not in ourselves, neither in our nature. Therefore, if we find no certainty in things on earth, we must know that our salvation resteth upon God; and that he holdeth it in such a manner, that it can never vanish away. This is a very happy consideration.

If I see a man become wicked, what can I say for myself? I am so likewise; but I must come to this conclusion; though I am weak, God is steadfast and sure! Therefore, I must commit myself wholly into his hands. And for this cause our Lord Jesus informs us, John x. that those whom the Father hath given him, shall never perish. And why so? Because God the Father is stronger and more mighty than all those that would oppose him, or endeavour to prevent him from executing his will.

By these words he warneth us, that if we put our trust in ourselves, we shall be utterly dismayed; and indeed, we should be liable to perish every minute, if we were not upheld and maintained by a higher power than our own. But, as the mighty power of God cannot be overcome, our salvation resteth sure; for God keepeth it. Yea, (and as I said before,) Jesus Christ hath taken charge of our souls, and will not suffer us to be taken out of his hands. Although the devil may do what he can, though he use ever so many means, although it may seem a hundred thousand times as though we should be taken by violence out of the hands of our Lord Jesus Christ, yet notwithstanding, we shall remain there forever. And why so? Because our salvation is settled upon the election of God, and his unchangeable counsel.

Let us beware and take heed, when we see others stumble and fall from the gospel. Let us observe what St. John saith in chapter ii.; those that went from us, were not of us; otherwise they could never have been separated from us. We must know that God suffered hypocrites to remain among us for a season, although he knew they were reprobates. Our Lord Jesus plainly showeth that the faithful ought not to be troubled through the unthankfulness of men, when they rebel against the gospel; for they are grieved at the true doctrine, and are at defiance with God. Jesus Christ saith, every tree which God the Father hath not planted, shall be rooted up.

He compareth those who seem to be of the number of the faithful, to trees that are planted in a field or garden. Those that are open enemies to God, bear no resemblance to trees: but the hypocrites, who make a fair show, and would be taken for God's children, seem to be like trees planted in a field or garden; but they take no root, because God did not plant them: that is to say, he did not choose them. In order to try us, he suffereth them to pretend the name of God falsely; yet notwithstanding, he never adopted them for his children, neither are they chosen to the inheritance of life; therefore they must be plucked up.

If any one becomes dissatisfied with the gospel, men will say, behold, such a man hath fallen away. If there fall out any stumbling-block, (I speak not of those who show themselves open enemies to God, and manifestly contemn his word,) if there be any who are proud and lofty, who cannot abide sound doctrine, who reject it, and are grieved with it, they become a stumbling-block. Therefore the disciple asked our Lord Jesus Christ, why the Scribes and Pharisees were not edified: let them alone, saith he, they are blind. But beware ye, go not to destruction with them.

We must know that *all* are not elected and chosen of God the Father. Some will say, there is nothing but holiness in them; but this is a mistake; for it is evident that they never had any fear of God before their eyes; but are hypocrites. Therefore we must not be dismayed, if we see rebellion in men; for all are not planted by the hand of God. Thus we see how we must make our profit of this doctrine. We must know, first of all, that faith is given us from above: God having lightened us by his holy spirit, we receive the gospel; yet not by our own wit and virtue.

God giveth us this grace, because he had chosen us for his children, and adopted us before the beginning of the world: which is a singular and inestimable blessing, bestowed upon us, while others are left to perish. He was at liberty to choose whom he would: therefore it behooveth us to know that we are so much the more bound to him, because he hath delivered us out of the general destruction of mankind. Let us consider that it is very profitable for us to understand this free election of God, which maketh a difference between his children and the castaways.

When we see troubles and offences in the church, when we see those who had begun well turn aside from the true way, we must remember that men are frail; yet notwithstanding, we shall find sufficient sureness in our God; because he hath been graciously pleased to adopt us for his children; therefore he will keep us through Jesus Christ according to his promise. Let us resort to the election of God, whenever we become dismayed or cast down: if we see men fall away, if the whole church should seem to come to nought, we must remember that God hath his foundation; that is, the church is not grounded upon the will of men, for they did not make themselves, neither can they reform themselves: but this proceedeth from the pure goodness and mercy of God.

Although the upper part of the building be as it were overthrown, though we see no pillars, though the form and shape of it appear no more, yet God will keep the foundation sure, which never can be shaken. Thus the world may see whether the doctrine of God's election which we preach, be needless or not. We must not presume to enter into the secret counsel of God, to thoroughly comprehend his wonderful secrets; but if this be hid from us, to know that God chose us before the world was made, is it not to deprive us of a comfort which is not only profitable for us, but even necessary? The devil can find no better means to destroy our faith, than to hide this article from our view.

What case should we be in, and especially now-a-days, when there are so many rebels and hypocrites in the world? yea, and such, as men are looking for wonders at their hands. Might we not fear the same would befall us? How can we rest ourselves with constancy upon God, and commit ourselves to him with settled hearts, not doubting but that he will take care of us to the end, unless we flee to this election as our only refuge? If this is not true, it seemeth that God hath broken his promise, which was given us respecting his gospel; and that Jesus Christ is banished out of the world.

This is the principal cause, and the best means that satan can devise, to destroy our love for the gospel. Therefore, let us hold fast these weapons, in despite of satan and all his imps: for these must be our defence. Let us be confirmed in the election of our God, and make it available; and see that it be not taken from us; if we love the salvation of our own souls, let us attend well to these things. We must consider those who would hide such a doctrine from us our mortal enemies: the devil stirreth them up to deprive us of a comfort, which if we do not enjoy, we cannot be assured of our salvation. However, we must remember this exhortation of the apostle Paul; *let every one that nameth the name of Christ depart from iniquity.*

As the election of God is to give us a sure constancy, to make us happy in the midst of trouble, which otherwise might disquiet us, we must not cease to call upon him, to run to him, and to walk diligently in the way wherein he hath called us. There is a great difference between the assurance of the faithful, who are thoroughly persuaded of the surety of their salvation, and those who are negligent and careless, and think no harm can overtake them: these are as blocks; they know not the danger that surroundeth them, which should induce them to flee to God for protection: but on the contrary, after they have been once instructed, they never pay any more attention to doctrine.

But the faithful cease not to fear, although they

are grounded upon the goodness of God, and are persuaded that no storm nor tempest whatsoever can carry them away: yet notwithstanding, they continue to watch against the assaults of satan. They know their frailty, which causes them to put their trust in God, and pray to him, that he would not forsake them in time of need, but that he would put forth his hand and preserve them: they consider whereunto they are called; they repent, and call upon God to increase the graces of his holy spirit in them, and take from them their afflictions.

St. Paul saith, 1 Cor. x. 12. "Let him that thinketh he standeth take heed lest he fall." Not that St. Paul meant to put us in doubt, or cause us to waver; as though we knew not what to do, nor whether God would guide us to the end or not; for we must be thoroughly resolved upon this point, that the work which God hath begun, will be brought to perfection; as it is said in Phil. i. and likewise in many other places. We must call upon God, and stir up ourselves to daily prayer, that we may not abuse his grace. We must dedicate ourselves to him, we must walk in fear and carefulness, and beware that we be not entrapped in the condemnation of the wicked.

If they be poor blind creatures, we need not marvel to think they go astray: but seeing God hath enlightened us, doth it not behoove us to walk uprightly? Seeing he hath adopted us for his children, are we not under an obligation to serve and honour him as our Father? This is what St. Paul exhorteth us to do, when he saith, *let every one that nameth the name of Christ depart from iniquity.* To call upon the name of Christ, is to avouch ourselves to be his followers. When we speak of calling upon God, it meaneth, to pray to him, and implore his blessings: we likewise call upon the name of God, when we make profession to be of his people, and his church.

Therefore, we cannot take the name of christian

upon us, we cannot make protestation that we are of the company of the children of God, that we are of his church and people, to be short, we can have nothing to do with Christ, unless we be delivered from all our filthiness. If a man should call himself the servant of a prince, and in the mean time be a thief, ought he not to be doubly punished, because he abused the name that in no wise belonged to him? Behold the Son of God, who is the fountain of all holiness and righteousness! shall we endeavour to hide ourselves, and cloak all our filthiness, be it ever so shameful, under his name? Is not this such horrible sacrilege, that it deserveth the most severe punishment? It is true, that let us take whatsoever pains we may to serve God purely, we cease not to be wretched sinners, full of blemishes; and to have many wicked imperfections in us.

But if we desire to do well, if we hate sin, though we go limpingly, seeing our design is good, and we strive to go forward in the fear of God, and in obedience to his will, this is a right affection; and Jesus Christ maketh the same account of us, as though we were just; he freeth us from all our faults, and charges them not to our account. Therefore, the faithful, though they be not entirely perfect, though they have many sins, are taken for God's children; and Jesus Christ thinketh it no dishonour that they should be called by his name: for he causeth the goodness which is in them, through his grace, to be acceptable to God.

But if we abuse the name of Jesus Christ, and make a cloak of it for our sins, do we not deserve to have him rise up against us, seeing we have dishonoured his majesty, and falsified his name? Therefore, let us mark well what this word, *christianity*, meaneth: its meaning, is to be members of the Son of God! Christ having been pleased to accept us, we must cleave to him in all righteousness; for he hath received all fulness, that he might make us partakers of his grace. The spirit of God must reign in us, if we would be taken for his children, and for members of the Lord Jesus Christ.

All those that give themselves to wickedness, and submit not themselves to the will of God, to mortify their wicked lusts, are false varlets and abusers, in pretending to claim the name of christians. When we see men separate themselves from the church of God, when we see those who have begun well, go not on, we must remember that although there be weakness in men, the foundation of God ceaseth not to remain sure. And how so? Because God knoweth whom he hath chosen, and will certainly maintain them. Therefore, let us not doubt but what we are of that number, seeing our Lord hath called us to him ; for this is a witness that he had chosen us before we were born : then let us content ourselves with this holy calling.

Let us not be troubled with whatever stumbling-blocks may fall in our way ; but in the mean time, let us hope that we shall be preserved by the power of God, and that he will maintain his church, and not suffer his people to perish ; although the world may strive hard to lessen their number. Let us study to walk in fear, not abusing the will of our God ; but know, seeing he hath separated us from the rest of the world, that we must live as children in his house : for he hath given us the outward mark of baptism, that we may have the seal of the Holy Ghost. This is the *earnest* (as St. Paul calleth it, Eph. i. 14.) of our election : it is the pledge which we have of our being called to the heavenly inheritance.

Therefore, let us pray to God, that he would sign and seal his free election in our hearts by his holy spirit ; that he would shelter us under the shadow of his wings : and if the poor castaways go astray, and are carried away by the devil ; if they fall, never to rise again ; if they cast themselves headlong into destruction, let us pray God to keep us under his protection, that we may be in subjection to his will, and be maintained by his power. Although the world strive to shake us, still let us rest ourselves upon this foundation ; *The Lord knoweth them that are his:* and let us never be put from it, but stand steadfastly to it, and profit more and more by it, until God take us to his kingdom, which is not subject to any changes.

SERMON VII.

1 TIMOTHY, Chap. ii. *verses* 3, 4, *and* 5.

3. For this is good and acceptable in the sight of God our Saviour:
4. Who will have all men to be saved, and to come unto the knowledge of the truth.
5. For there is one God, and one mediator between God and men, the man Christ Jesus.

WHEN we despise those whom God would have honoured, it is as much as if we should despise him : so it is, if we make no account of the salvation of those whom God calleth to himself. For it seemeth thereby, that we would stay him from showing his mercy to poor sinners, who are in the way to ruin. The reason why St. Paul useth this argument, *that God will have all the world to be saved*, is, that we may, as much as lieth in us, also seek the salvation of those, who seem to be banished from the kingdom of God; especially while they are unbelievers.

We must always observe what the condition of the world was in the days of St. Paul. It was something new and strange to have the gospel published to the world in those days: for it appeared that God had chosen the stock of Abraham, and that the rest of the world would be deprived of all hope of salvation. And indeed we see how holy writ setteth forth the adoption of this people : but St. Paul commandeth us to pray for all the world ; and not without cause ; for he addeth the reason, which is here mentioned : to wit, because *God will have all men to be saved.* As if he should say, my friends, it is reasonable that we should observe what the will of God is, and at what he aimeth ; that every one of us may employ himself to serve him aright.

Therefore, seeing it is the will of God, that all men should be partakers of that salvation which he hath sent in the person of his only begotten Son, we must endeavour to draw poor, silly, ignorant creatures, to us, that we may all come together, to this inheritance of the kingdom of heaven, which hath been promised us. But we must observe, that St. Paul speaketh not of every particular man, but of all sorts of men, and of all people. Therefore, when he saith that God will have all men to be saved, we must not think that he speaketh of them individually, but his meaning is this ; that whereas in times past he chose a certain people to himself, he meaneth now to show mercy to all the world ; yea, even to them that seemed to be shut out from the hope of salvation.

He saith in another place, the heathens were with out God, and void of all promise ; because they were not as yet brought to the fellowship of the Jews. This was a special privilege that God had given to the descendants of Abraham. Therefore St. Paul's meaning is, not that God will save every man, but that the promises which were given to but one people, are now extended to all the world : for as he saith in this same epistle, the wall was broken down at the coming of our Lord Jesus Christ. God had separated the Jews from all other nations; but when Jesus Christ appeared for the salvation of the world, then was this difference, which existed between them and the Gentiles, taken away.

Therefore, God will now embrace us all : and this

is the entrance into our salvation. For if that had always continued, which God ordained but for a season, then should we be all accursed; and the gospel would not have been preached to us: we should have had no sign or token of the love and goodness of God. But now we have become his children; we are no more strangers to the promises, as were our fathers: for Jesus Christ came to be a Saviour to all in general; he offered the grace of God the Father, that all might receive it.

As St. Paul speaketh of all nations, so he likewise speaketh of all conditions; as if he should say, God will save kings and magistrates, as well as others: we must not restrain his fatherly goodness to ourselves alone, nor to any certain number of people. And why so? For he showeth that he will be favourable to all: thus we have St. Paul's meaning. To confirm this matter, he addeth, it is God's will that all should come to the knowledge of the truth. We must mark well why St. Paul useth this argument; for we cannot know the will of God, unless it be made known to us; unless we have some sign or token whereby we may perceive it. It is too high a matter for us to know what God's counsel is; but as far as he showeth it to us by effect, so far we comprehend it.

The gospel is called the mighty power of God, and salvation to all them that believe: yea, it is the gate of paradise. It followeth then, if through the will of God the gospel be preached to all the world, there is a token that salvation is common to all. Thus St. Paul proveth, that God's will is that all men should be saved. He hath not appointed his apostles to proclaim his name only among the Jews, for we know that the commission was given them to preach to all creatures; to be witnesses of Jesus Christ from Jerusalem to Samaria, and from thence throughout all the world.

Are the apostles sent to publish the truth of God

to all people, and to all conditions of men? It followeth then, that God presenteth himself to all the world : that the promise belongeth to both great and small ; as well to the Gentiles now, as to the Jews before. But before we go any farther, it is necessary to beat down the folly, or rather the beastliness of those, who abuse this passage of St. Paul ; who endeavour to make the election of God of no effect, and to utterly take it away. They say, if God will have all men to be saved, it follows, that he hath not chosen a certain number of mankind, and cast the rest away, but that his will remaineth indifferent.

They pretend that it is left to the choice of men to save themselves or not ; that God letteth us alone, and waiteth to see whether we will come to him or not ; and so receiveth them that come unto him. But in the mean time, they destroy the ground work of our salvation ; for we know that we are so accursed, that the inheritance of salvation is far from us : if we say that Jesus Christ hath come to remedy that, then must we examine the nature of mankind. We are so contrary in our nature, and such enemies to God, that we cannot but resist him : we are so given to evil and wickedness, that we cannot so much as conceive a good thought. How then can it be, that we may become partakers of that salvation which is offered in the gospel, unless God draw us to it by his holy spirit? Let us now see whether God draw all the world to it or not. No, no; for then had our Lord Jesus Christ said in vain, " No man can come to me, except the Father, which hath sent me, draw him." John vi. 44. So then we must needs conclude, that it is a special grace that God bestoweth upon such as pleaseth him, to draw them, and teach them in such a manner, that they believe the gospel, and receive it with true faith.

And now, why doth God choose one, and leave another? We know that men cannot come to God by their own deserts, neither are those, who have been chosen, deserving any such thing as to be preferred to their companions; as though there were some worthiness in them. It followeth then, that before the world was made, (as St. Paul saith in the first to the Ephesians,) God chose such as pleased him: and we know not why this man was chosen in preference to that. And still we must confess that whatsoever God doth, is done justly; although we cannot comprehend it. Therefore, let us receive that whereof we are so thoroughly certified in holy writ; and not suffer ourselves to be lead astray, under a shadow of vain reason, used by men, who are ignorant of the word of God.

At the first sight, there appears to be some weight in their argument; *God will have all men to be saved:* therefore say they, it is left to the free choice of every man to become enlightened in the faith, and to partake of salvation. If a man will read but three lines, he will easily perceive, that St. Paul here speaketh not of every particular man, (as we have already shown,) but that he speaketh of all people, and of all conditions of men. He showeth that the case standeth not as it did before the coming of Christ, when there was but one chosen people, but that God now showeth himself a Saviour to all the world; as it is said, thine inheritance shall be even to the ends of the earth.

Moreover, that no man may abuse himself, or be deceived by the vain and foolish talk of those who pervert holy writ, let us examine how the doctrine of these enemies of God, and all godliness, standeth. God will have all men to be saved; that is, as they imagine, every one. If it be the will of God at present, no doubt it was the same from the beginning of the world: for we know that his mind changeth not. So then, if at this day God will have all men to be saved, his mind was so always; and if his mind was so always, what shall we make of what St. Paul saith? that he will that all men come to the knowledge of the truth. He chose but one people to himself, as it is said, Acts xiv.; and left the poor Gentiles to walk in their own ignorance.

There were likewise some countries where he would not suffer St. Paul to preach; as in Bithynia and Phrygia; Acts xvi. 7. And so we see that God would not have the knowledge of the gospel to come to every one at first. Thus we may easily see the errour of those, who abuse this text. St. Paul speaketh not in this place of the counsel of God, neither doth he mean to lead us to his everlasting election, which was before the beginning of the world: but only showeth what his will and pleasure is, as far as we ought to know it.

It is true that God changeth not; neither hath he two wills; nor doth he use any counterfeit dealing: and yet the scripture speaketh unto us in two ways, concerning his will. And how can that be? How cometh it to pass that his will is spoken of in two different ways? It is because of our grossness, and want of understanding. Why doth he make himself to have eyes, to have ears, and to have a nose? Why doth he take upon him men's affections? Why is it that he saith he is angry, he is sorry? Is it not because we cannot comprehend him in his incomprehensible majesty? Therefore, it is not absurd that holy writ should speak unto us of the will of God after two sorts: not because his will is double, but in order that he may apply himself to our weakness, knowing that our understanding is gross and heavy.

When the scripture informeth us that God hath chosen such as pleased him before the world began, we behold a counsel into which we cannot enter. Why then doth holy writ inform us that this election and choice of God is everlasting? It is not without cause; for it is a very profitable doctrine, if it be received as it ought to be. For thereby we are reminded, that we are not called to the knowledge of the gospel by reason of our own worthiness. We are no better than others, for we all sprung from the cursed root of Adam; we are all subject to the same condemnation; and we are all shut up under the slavery of sin and death.

When it pleased God to draw us out of the darkness of unbelief, and give us the light of the gospel, he looked not at any service which we might have performed, or at any virtue we might have possessed; but he called us, having chosen us before. This is the order in which St. Paul maketh mention in Romans viii.; that knowing God, we must not take the glory to ourselves. Thus, the calling of the faithful resteth upon this counsel of God; and we see how far the Lord maketh known to us, that which he had decreed before we were born. He toucheth us with his holy spirit, and we are ingrafted, as it were, into the body of our Lord Jesus Christ. This is the true *earnest* of our adoption: this is the pledge given us, to put us out of all doubt that God taketh and holdeth us for his children, when by faith we are made one with Jesus Christ, who is the only begotten Son of God; unto whom belongeth the inheritance of life.

God giveth us such a sure testimony of his will, that notwithstanding our ignorance, he putteth us out of doubt of our election; he giveth us a hope, of which we should be entirely void, if Jesus Christ did not call us to be members of his body. Thus we see how profitable this doctrine of election is to us: it serveth to humble us, knowing that our salvation hangeth not upon our deserts, neither upon the virtue which God might have found in us: but upon the election that was made before we were born; before we could do either good or evil.

When we know, that according to this unchangeable election, God hath called us to himself, we are so much the more put out of doubt of our salvation. Jesus Christ saith, no man taketh from me that which the Father hath given me: John x. What is it that the Father hath given Jesus Christ? They whom he hath chosen, and whom he knoweth to be his. Seeing the case standeth thus, that God hath given us to his Son, to be kept and defended by him, and that Jesus Christ promiseth that none of us shall be lost, but that he will exercise all the might and power of the Godhead to save and defend us, is not this a comfort surpassing all the treasures of the world? Is not this the true ground upon which all the assurance and certainty of our salvation is settled?

We are as birds upon the boughs, and set forth as a prey to satan. What assurance then could we have of to-morrow, and of all our life; yea, and after death, were it not that God, who hath called us, will end his work as he hath begun it. How hath he gathered us together in the faith of his gospel? Is it grounded upon us? Nay, entirely to the contrary; it proceedeth from his free election. Therefore we may be so much the more freed from doubt. We must not strive to know any more of God's counsel, than what is revealed in holy writ.

The will of God is opened to us, as often as we hear his word preached; whereby he calleth and exhorteth us all to repentance. After he hath once shown us that we are all damned in his sight, and that there is nothing but condemnation in us, he showeth us that we must renounce ourselves, and get out of this bottomless pit. In that which God exhorteth all men, we may judge that it is his will that all men should be saved: as he saith by the prophet Ezekiel, xviii. 23. " Have I any pleasure at all that the wicked should die? saith the Lord God; and not that he should return from his ways and live?" And again, chap. xxxiii. 11. "Say unto them, As I live, saith the Lord God, I have no pleasure in the death of the wicked; but that the wicked turn from his way and live."

How will God have sinners turn themselves? and how shall we know it? Seeing he will have repentance preached to all the world. When it is said that God will have mercy upon sinners, upon such as will come to him, and ask forgiveness in Christ's name, it is a general doctrine. So then, it is said, that God will have all men to be saved; not having respect to what we devise or imagine, that is, as far as our knowledge can comprehend it. When the scripture speaketh of the love and will of God, let us see if men can have repentance by their own actions, being self taught, or whether it is God that giveth it.

God saith by his prophet, I will that all men turn and live. Can a man by his own works turn himself? No: for if that were in our power, it were more than to make us. It is an undoubted doctrine throughout the whole scripture, that our Lord Jesus Christ giveth himself the praise of turning us. He saith, Ezekiel xi. 19. "I will put a new spirit within you: and I will take the stony heart out of their flesh, and will give them an heart of flesh." To be short, there is nothing that the faithful ought so much to do, as to give God the glory, confessing that it is he alone that can turn us: and that he hath adopted us in such a manner, that he must needs draw us by the grace of his holy spirit.

Have men such knowledge that they are able to attain this faith, this wonderful wisdom which is contained in the gospel, such as the very angels themselves reverence? Let us mark what God saith to us in his word; that he will open our eyes, and unstop our ears: because the natural man understandeth no part of the secrets of God; for it is the Holy

Ghost that revealeth them to us. It is hardly possible to read a single passage in holy writ, without finding some sentence, which informeth us that men are utterly blind by nature, until God openeth their eyes. They can in no wise come to him, until he draw them, and enlighten them by his holy spirit.

Seeing that God alone turneth men from their wickedness, experience teacheth us, and so doth the holy scripture, that he giveth not his grace to all men. It is said, Deut. xxix. 4. "The Lord hath not given you an heart to perceive, and eyes to see, and ears to hear, unto this day." It is plainly shown that God doth not cast forth his grace without direction: but that it is only for those whom he hath chosen; for those that are of the body of his church, and of his flock. Thus we see what St. Paul meaneth, when he saith, *God will have all men to be saved:* that is, he will have some of all nations, and all conditions.

It is said that he offereth his gospel to all, which is the means of drawing us to salvation. And doth this profit all men? No; of this our own eyes are witnesses. For when we hear the truth of God, if we rebel against it, it proves a great condemnation to us. Yet so it is, that there are many, who do not profit by the gospel, but rather become worse; even those to whom it is preached; therefore, they are not all saved. God must go farther in order to bring us to salvation; he must not only appoint men, and send them to teach us faithfully, but he must operate upon our hearts, he must touch us to the quick, he must draw us to him, he must make his work profitable to us, and cause it to take root in our hearts.

It is evident that we have to consider the will of God in two ways: not that it is double of itself, (as we before observed,) but we must consider it as adapted to our weakness. He formeth his speech to us in his word, according to our capacity. If God should speak according to his majesty, his speech would be beyond our comprehension; it would utterly confound us! For if our eyes be not able to abide the brightness of the sun, would our minds be able to comprehend the infinite majesty of God? These silly men, who would destroy God's election, ought not to abuse this passage; nor say that we make God to have two wills; for therein do they impudently misrepresent us. We say, as far as we can perceive, God would have all men to be saved; whensoever, and how oft soever, he appointeth his gospel to be preached to us.

As we said before, the gate of paradise is opened to us, when we are called to be partakers of that redemption which was purchased for us by our Lord Jesus Christ. And this is the will of God, as far as we can comprehend it; that when he exhorteth us to repentance, he is ready to receive us, if we will come to him. Although we have answered the doubts which might have been raised upon this subject, we will bring a similitude to make this doctrine more easy. (I call a similitude, that agreement and similarity which God maketh between the children of Israel and us.) God saith, Deut. vii. that he chose the children of Abraham for his inheritance, and dedicated them to himself: he loved them, and took them for his own household.

This is true; for he made his covenant with all those that were circumcised. Was circumcision a vain figure, and of no importance? Nay, it was a sure and undoubted sign that God had chosen that people for his own: accounting all for his flock that came of that race. And yet, was there not a special grace for some of that people? Surely there was, as St. Paul setteth forth, Romans ix. 6, 7. "For they are not all Israel which are of Israel: neither because they are the seed of Abraham, are they all children;" for God deprived some of this benefit, that his grace and goodness might seem greater to those whom he called to himself. Behold, therefore, the will of God which was made manifest to the children of Israel, is at this day made manifest to us.

It is said in Amos iv. 7. " God caused it to rain upon one city, and caused it not to rain upon another city." So the Lord sendeth his gospel wheresoever it pleaseth him : his grace is poured out upon all the world ; yet it cannot be but he worketh otherwise with those whom he draweth to himself : for all of us have our ears stopped, and our eyes hoodwinked. We are deaf and blind, unless he prepareth us to receive his word. When the gospel is preached to us, it is as much as if God reached out his hand, (as he saith in Isa. lxv. 2.) and said to us, come unto me. It is a matter which ought to touch us to the heart, when we perceive that God cometh to seek us ; he doth not wait till we come to him, but he showeth us that he is ready to receive us, although we were his deadly enemies. He wipeth away all our faults, and maketh us partakers of that salvation, which was purchased for us by our Lord Jesus Christ.

Thus we see how worthy the gospel is to be esteemed, and what a treasure it is ! As St. Paul saith to the Romans ; " It is the power of God unto salvation to every one that believeth :" it is the kingdom of heaven ; and God openeth the door, that we, being taken out of the bottomless pit wherein we were sunk by nature, may enter into his glory. We must remember that it is not enough for us to receive the word that is preached to us by the mouth of man, but after we have heard it, God must speak to us inwardly by his holy spirit ; for this is the only means to bring us to the knowledge of the truth. Therefore, when God hath dealt so mercifully with us, as to give us the light of faith, let us hold it fast, and pray him to continue it, and bring his work to perfection.

Let us not lift ourselves proudly above other men, as though we were more worthy than they are, for we know that it is our God that hath chosen us, and setteth us apart from others, by his mere goodness and free mercy. We must know, moreover, that men are very faulty, when God offereth them his word, and they receive it not. This is spoken that unbelievers and rebels might have their mouths stopped, that they might not blaspheme the name of God, as though he had been wanting on his part; and to the end, that all the faithful should, in humbleness of heart, glorify God for his grace and mercy toward them; for we see how he calleth all those to whom his word is preached, to salvation.

If men reply, by saying, they cannot come to God; we cannot stand to plead here, for we shall always find ourselves in fault. If a man say, it resteth only in the hands of God, and if he would give me repentance, could he not do it! If I remain stiff-necked in my hardness and malice, what can I do in this case, seeing God will not give me repentance to turn to him? This is not in any wise to be allowed; for God calleth us sufficiently to him, and we cannot accuse him of cruelty; even if we had not his word, we must needs confess that he is just, although we know not the cause that moved him to deprive us of it.

When we are called to come to God, and know that he is ready to receive us, if we do not come, can we deny that we are unthankful? Let us not separate salvation from the knowledge of the truth; for God doth not mean to lie, nor deceive men, when he saith, when they come to the knowledge of the truth they shall be saved. *God will have all men to be saved;* but how? *If they will come to the knowledge of the truth.* Every man would be saved, but no man will draw nigh to God. The scripture informeth us, that if we desire salvation, we must attend to the means which God hath appointed; that is, we must receive his word with obedience and faith.

The scripture saith, this is everlasting life; to wit, to know God the Father, and to receive Christ as our only Saviour. Therefore let us learn, as it is here set forth, not to doubt of the certainty of our salvation; for the kingdom of God is within us. If we wish God to receive us, we must receive the doctrine given us by St. Paul. How are we called to the hope of salvation? By the influence of the grace of God, which maketh known to us his love and favour. Thus we may see what St. Paul's meaning is, when he saith, God will have his grace made known to all the world, and his gospel preached to all creatures. Therefore, we must endeavour, as much as possible, to persuade those who are strangers to the faith, and seem to be utterly deprived of the goodness of God, to accept of salvation.

Jesus Christ is not only a Saviour of few, but he offereth himself to all. As often as the gospel is preached to us, we ought to consider that God calleth us to him; and if we attend to this call, it shall not be in vain, neither shall it be lost labour. But can we come to him without any assistance, except what we derive from our own nature? Alas, we cannot! "Because the carnal mind is enmity against God; for it is not subject to the law of God, neither indeed can be." Romans viii. 7. When God dealeth so graciously with us, as to touch our hearts with his holy spirit, then he causeth his gospel to work profitably to our salvation; then he maketh a display of the virtue spoken of by St. Paul.

Again, we must remember when the gospel is preached to us, that it is to make us more void of excuse. Seeing God hath already shown us that he was ready to receive us to mercy, if we would come unto him, our condemnation will no doubt be increased, if we be so wicked as to draw back, when he calleth so mildly and lovingly. Notwithstanding, (as we are here exhorted,) let us not leave off praying for all men in general; for St. Paul showeth that God will have all men to be saved; that is to say, men of all people and nations.

Although we see a great diversity among men, yet we must not forget that God hath made us all in his own image and likeness, and that we are the workmanship of his hand: therefore he extends his goodness to those who are afar off, of which we have had sufficient proof: for when he drew us unto him, were we not his enemies? How then cometh it to pass that we are now of the household of faith, the children of God, and members of our Lord Jesus Christ? Is it not because he hath gathered us to himself? And is he not the Saviour of the whole world, as well as of us? Did Jesus Christ come to be the mediator of two or three men only? No, no; but he is the *mediator between God and men.*

Therefore, we may be so much the more assured that God taketh and holdeth us for his children, if we endeavour to bring those to him who are afar off. Let us comfort ourselves, and take courage in this our calling: although there be at this day a great forlornness, though we seem to be miserable creatures, utterly cast away and condemned, yet we must labour as much as possible, to draw those to salvation who seem to be afar off. And above all things, let us pray to God for them, waiting patiently till it please him to show his good will toward them, as he hath shown it to us.

SERMON VIII.

1 TIMOTHY, Chap. iii. *verses* 14 *and* 15.

14 These things write I unto thee, hoping to come unto thee shortly:
15 But if I tarry long, that thou mayest know how thou oughtest to behave thyself in the house of God, which is the church of the living God, the pillar and ground of the truth.

WE see what holiness and perfection St. Paul required in all those that had any public charge in the church of God : we see also how he concluded that those who behaved themselves well and faithfully in office, " purchased to themselves a good degree, and great boldness in the faith which is in Jesus Christ." When there is good order in the church, and the children of God do their duty faithfully, it is an honour to them ; and men think them worthy of reverence. This is not to puff them up, and make them proud, but that they may be more and more enabled to serve God ; and that men may more willingly hear them, and receive counsel and advice from them : this is the meaning of St. Paul.

Those that do not their duty as they ought, have their mouths stopped ; they can do nothing with the people, but are worthily mocked : although they are bold, yet they have no gravity ; therefore their doctrine cannot be received. Those that are called to fill offices in the church of God, must strive so much the more to do well ; and endeavour to serve God, and the people of God, faithfully. But now-a-days, the wicked seem to bear the sway ; before whom, the world, as it were, trembles.

Thus we see that things are much out of order among us. Where is our liberty at the present day ? Not in the faith, but in all wickedness ; among those that are hardened and past all shame. We see good men oppressed, who dare not speak in their own defence. If a man reprove sin, and go about to redress matters, and set them in order, he is beset on all sides by the wicked. We see not many that trouble themselves to maintain a good cause, for every man betrayeth the truth. We suffer things to go as evil as they can; these are the days spoken of by the prophet Isaiah; righteousness and justice are hunted out from among us; and there is no man that hath zeal enough to set himself against wickedness. It may well seem that we have conspired to foster wickedness, and bring it to full maturity.

The wrath of God is kindled against us; all things are out of order. Those that walk as becometh christians, and labour to serve God purely, are marked out as enemies; and men seek to trample them under foot. On the other hand, we see the wicked do what they list; they act as wild beasts: yet men stand in fear of them; and this liberty that is given them, maketh them the more hardened. When we see such disorder, have we not reason to sigh and be ashamed of ourselves, knowing that God doth not rule at all among us, but that the devil hath full possession? Shall we boast that we have the gospel? It is true, his word is preached among us, but do we not see that it is contemned, and that men make a mock of it? But let them flatter themselves in hardening their hearts against God; yet notwithstanding, this doctrine will continue, and will be preached for a witness against us in the latter day, unless the Lord come speedily and reform us.

St. Paul writeth these things to Timothy, that if he tarry long, before he come, he may know how to behave himself in the house of God. Here St. Paul exhorteth Timothy, and in his person all the faithful, to walk warily and carefully in conformity to the spiritual government of the church. For the house of God, if he dwell therein, is the upholder of the truth. Therefore it is no trifling matter to be called of the Lord, to serve him in the office spoken of by St. Paul. We must beware and fail not, seeing God bestoweth upon us the honour of governing his house : yea, that house wherein he hath his abode, and will make known his majesty : which is, as it were, a closet where his truth is kept, that it may be maintained and preserved in the world. If the matter stand thus, have not those whom God hath thus honoured, great occasion to be watchful, and to endeavour to execute the charge committed to them ? Thus we see St. Paul's meaning.

But before we go any farther, it will be necessary to put aside the impudency of the *papists*, who abuse this text, in order to establish their own tyranny. For if they can once set up the church of God, they think they have won the field. But they should first prove that theirs is the church of God ; which is so difficult a matter for them to do, that the contrary is evident. And why so ? Because St. Paul saith, the church is the house of God. They have driven our Lord Jesus Christ out of doors, so that he reigneth no more among them as ruler, whereto he was appointed by the Father ; who requireth that we should do him homage, submitting ourselves wholly to his doctrine.

Do the papists suffer Jesus Christ to govern them purely and peaceably ? Nay, I am sure they do not. They coin and stamp whatever they think proper : and whatsoever they decree, is taken for articles of belief. They mingle and confound the doctrine of the gospel, with notions devised by themselves : so that we may easily see, it is not God's house : otherwise Jesus Christ would not be banished therefrom. Moreover, St. Paul addeth, the church must uphold the truth. But we see in these times, that it is oppressed by the tyranny of the *pope* ; where there remaineth nothing but lies, errours, corruption, and idolatry. Seeing this is the case, we may well conclude that theirs is not the true church of God.

But we will go farther. It was not the meaning of St. Paul, (as the papists imagine,) that the church cannot err because it is governed by the Holy Ghost, and that whatsoever they think good, must be received. But on the contrary, St. Paul observes, that the church is the upholder of the truth; because God will have his truth preached by the mouth of men; therefore he hath appointed the ministration of his word, that we might know his will; for God useth this mean, that men may know his truth, and reverence it from age to age. This is the reason why the church is called a pillar.

The papists endeavour to bury the doctrine of the gospel, when they say, the church cannot err. Let us consider, say they, that God will inspire us; yet in the mean time they leave the word of God, thinking they may wander here and there, without committing evil. And why? Oh, the church cannot err. But on the other hand, let us see upon what condition our Lord hath honoured his church. St. Paul informeth us, that he doth not bind us to devise what we think good, but he holdeth us tied and bound to his word; as it is said, Isa. li. 16. "I have put my words in thy mouth, and have covered thee in the shadow of mine hand, that I may plant the heavens, and lay the foundations of the earth, and say unto Zion, Thou art my people."

How is it that God promiseth that he will reign in the midst of his people? He doth not say, because he inspireth them, that they have leave to coin new articles of faith! No, no: but he saith, he will put the words of our Lord Jesus Christ into the mouths of such as must preach his name. For that promise was not made for the time of the law only, but is proper for the church of Christ; and shall continue to the end of the world. Thus we see how the church must be the pillar to bear up the truth of God.

God will not come down from heaven, neither will he send his angels to bring us revelations from above; but he will be made known to us by his word. Therefore, he will have ministers of the church preach his truth, and instruct us therein. If we attend not to these things, we are not the church of God; but are guilty, as much as lieth in us, of abolishing his truth; we are traitors and murderers. And why so? Because God could maintain his truth otherwise if he would: he is not bound to these means, neither hath he any need of the help of men. But he will have his truth made known by such preaching as he hath commanded. What then would become of us, if we should leave off this preaching? should we not thereby endeavour to bring this truth to nought? It is said, the gospel, (as it is preached,) "is the power of God unto salvation to every one that believeth." Romans i. 16.

And how so? Is it because God hath no other means, but by the voice of men? in this sound that vanisheth away in the air? No, no; but yet he hath appointed this means, to the end that when we are restored by his grace, we may attend to the hearing of his word with all reverence: then shall we feel that his doctrine is not vain and unprofitable, but hath its effect, and is of such efficacy, as to call us to eternal life. For St. Paul saith, Romans x. 17. "Faith cometh by hearing:" and we know it is faith that quickeneth our souls, which otherwise would be helpless and lost. Thus let us mark well St. Paul's meaning, whereby we may know how impudent and beastly the papists are, to claim this text in order to establish their tyranny, which is entirely contrary to the meaning of the apostle.

But it is not enough to reprove the papists; *we*

also must be edified by the doctrine contained in the text. Therefore, first of all, those that have charge to preach the doctrine of the gospel, must take heed to themselves. And why so? Because they are set in God's house to govern it. If a man do any one the honour, to put the rule and government of his house and goods in his hands, ought he not to conduct himself in such a manner, as to please the one who committed this trust to him? If a prince make a man overseer of his household, is he not bound to do his duty faithfully? So the living God appointeth those that must preach his word in his house and temple: he will have them govern his people in his name, and bear the message of salvation. Seeing they are called to this high station, what carefulness and humility ought there to be in them!

Therefore, let those that are appointed ministers of the word of God, know that they have not only to do with men, but that they are accountable to him who hath called them to this high office: let them not be puffed up with the honour and dignity of their station, but know that they shall be so much the less able to excuse themselves, if they walk not uprightly: and that they commit horrible sacrilege, and shall have a fearful vengeance of God prepared for them, if they labour not to serve him as they ought.

First of all, we are exhorted to do our duty; God having honoured us, who were so unworthy, we ought to labour on our part, to fill the office whereunto we are called. When the church is called the house of the living God, it ought to awaken us to walk otherwise than we do. Why do we sleep in our sins? why do we run into wickedness? do we think that God doth not see us? that we are far out of his sight, and from the presence of our Lord Jesus Christ? Let us remember that the word of God is preached to us, that God dwelleth among us, and is present with us; as our Lord Jesus Christ saith,

Mat. xviii. 20. " Where two or three are gathered together in my name, there am I in the midst of them." And we know, as it is said, Col. ii. 9. that, " In him dwelleth all the fulness of the Godhead bodily."

So then, how oft soever the devil attempts to rock us to sleep, and tie us to the vanities of this world, or tempt us with wicked lusts, we ought to remember this sentence, and set it before our eyes ; *that God dwelleth in the midst of us, and that we are his house.* Now we must consider that God cannot dwell in a foul place : he must have a holy house and temple. And how ? Oh, there is no difficulty in setting out ourselves finely, that all the world may gaze at us : but God taketh no pleasure in all these vanities of the world. Our beautifying must be spiritual : we must be clad with the graces of the Holy Ghost : this is the gold and silver, these are the precious stones spoken of by the prophet Isaiah, when he describeth the temple of God, chap. lx. 6.

Seeing God is so gracious as to have his word preached among us, let us live in obedience to his divine commands, that he may reside with us, and we be his temple. For this cause, let us see that we cleanse ourselves from all our filthiness, and renounce it, that we may be a fit place for God's holiness to dwell in. If we attend to these things, we shall reap great joy ; seeing our Lord joineth himself to us, and maketh his residence in our souls and bodies. What are we ? There is nothing but rottenness in us : I speak not of the body only, but more particularly of the soul, which is still more infected : and yet we see the Lord will build us up, that we may be fit temples for his majesty to reside in. We have great occasion to rejoice by reason of this text ; and ought to strive to obtain the pureness which is required by the gospel ; because God will have us joined to him, and sanctified by his holy spirit.

Our text says, *the church of God is the pillar and ground of the truth.* God is not under the necessity of borrowing any thing from man, as we before observed; he can cause his truth to reign without our help: but he doth us this honour, and is so gracious as to employ us in this worthy and precious calling. He could instruct us without our hearing the voice of man; he could also send his angels, as he did to his servants in ancient times: but he calleth and gathereth us together in his church; there is his banner which he will set up among his flock; this is the kingly sceptre whereby he will have us ruled.

Therefore God hath shut up his truth in the scriptures, and will have it preached and expounded to us daily. For when St. Paul speaketh of the truth, he meaneth the doctrine of salvation, which God hath revealed to us in his word. The apostle saith, the doctrine of God, (which is the incorruptible seed, whereby we are born anew to everlasting life,) is the truth. This is set forth, Col. i. 5. John xvi. 13. and xvii. 17. St. John often speaketh of the gospel, by calling it the truth: as if he should say, without it we know nothing, and whatsoever we can comprehend, is vain: so that this is the only sure foundation upon which we can rest.

And indeed, what would it profit us if we knew all other things, and were destitute of the knowledge of our God? If we know not God, I say, alas, are we not more than miserable? But as God hath imprinted his image in his word, it is there he presenteth himself to us, and will have us to behold him, as it were, face to face. 2 Cor. iii. and iv. Therefore it is not in vain that St. Paul giveth this title to the preaching of the word of God; namely, *that it is the truth.* By this means he maketh himself known to us; it is also the means of our salvation: it is our life, our riches, and the seed whereby we become the children of God : in short, it is the nourishment of our souls, by which we are quickened.

Therefore let us remember that St. Paul saith, the truth is maintained among us by the preaching of the gospel; and men are appointed thereunto. First of all, we are miserable, (as I before observed,) if we know not God. And how shall we know him, unless we suffer ourselves to be taught by his word ? We must learn to seek for this treasure, and apply all our labour to find it : and when God is so gracious, as to offer it to us, let us receive it as poor beggars starved with hunger. When it pleaseth him to bestow such a benefit upon us, let us withdraw ourselves from worldly matters, that we may not despise his inestimable blessings.

Seeing the truth of God cannot reign among us, unless the gospel be preached, we ought to esteem it highly, knowing that he otherwise holdeth himself afar off. If these things were observed as they ought to be, we should see more reverence for the doctrine of the word of God. In these days we can hardly tell what the word *church* meaneth. It is true, men boast that the gospel is preached, and that there is a reformation according to the word of God; but while they use this word *church*, they know not what it means.

Some say, they believe there is a universal church ; but they speak in language which they do not understand. Such are the papists, who are so ignorant of the word *church*, being bewitched after the traditions of men, and bound by their tyranny, that they cannot understand it; neither dare they inquire what the church of God is. They have their foolish devotions, to which they are so much given, that they cannot be brought from them to the right way of salvation. As, for us, we have the word of God, but we hardly know how to maintain it. We see what contempt there is cast upon it, when it is preached among us, and how it is set at nought ; every man being his own teacher.

Many are glutted, as it were, with the gospel ; and think they know more than is necessary : they know so much, that they become sensible of their own condemnation. Thus they shall be twice guilty ; because they have once tasted the heavenly gifts, and are now such contemners of the word of God : we plainly perceive that they cast off all honesty, reverence, and religion and would be content to have God unknown among them. We ought to be greatly ashamed, seeing God hath so enlightened us, that we give ourselves to such wickedness ; and cause the gospel to be evil spoken of among the ignorant and unbelievers.

If we knew how to profit by what is contained in this place, we should have great reason to rejoice ; seeing God will have his truth maintained by the means of preaching. There is nothing in men but wickedness ; and yet God will use them for witnesses of his truth, having committed it to their keeping. Although there are but few that preach the word of God, yet notwithstanding, this treasure is common to the whole church. Therefore we are keepers of the truth of God ; that is to say, of his precious image, of that which concerneth the majesty of the doctrine of our salvation, and the life of the world.

When God calleth us to so honourable a charge, have we not great reason to rejoice and praise his holy name ? Let us remember to keep this treasure safe, that it be not profaned among us. St. Paul speaketh not only to instruct those that are called to preach the gospel, but that we may all know what blessings God hath bestowed upon us, when his word is preached in its purity. Our salvation is a matter of great importance ; and we must come to it by means of the gospel. For faith is the life of our souls : as the body is quickened by the soul, so is the soul by faith. So then we are dead, until God calleth us to the knowledge of his truth. Therefore we need not fear, for God will adopt us for his children, if we receive the doctrine of the gospel.

We need not soar above the clouds, we need not travel up and down the earth, we need not go beyond the seas, nor to the bottomless pit, to seek God; for we have his word in our hearts, and in our mouths. God openeth to us the door of paradise, when we hear the promises that are made to us in his name. It is as much as if he reached out his hand visibly, and received us for his children. God sealeth this doctrine by the signs which are annexed to it : for it is certain that the sacraments have a tendency to this end, that we may know that the church is the house of God, in which he is resident, and that his truth is maintained thereby.

When we are baptized in the name of our Lord Jesus Christ, we are brought into God's household : it is the mark of our adoption. Now, he cannot be our Father, unless we are under his divine protection, and governed by his holy spirit : as we have an evident witness in baptism, and a greater in the Lord's Supper : that is, we have a plain declaration that we are joined to God, and made one with him. For our Lord Jesus Christ showeth us that we are his body; that every one is a member: that he is the head whereby we are nourished with his substance and virtue. As the body is not separate from the head, so Jesus Christ showeth us that his life is common with ours, and that we are partakers of all his benefits.

When we behold this, is it not enough to make the truth of God precious to us ? Is it not a looking-glass, in which we may see that God not only dwelleth among us, but that he also dwelleth in every one of us ? God, having made us one with our Lord Jesus Christ, will not suffer us to be separated from him in any way whatsoever. Therefore, when we have this inestimable honour conferred upon us, should we not be ravished, as it were, and learn more and more to withdraw ourselves from the corruptions of this world, and truly show that it is not in vain that the Son of God will have us belong to him! How are we made one with our Lord Jesus Christ? By being pilgrims in this world, passing through it as true citizens of heaven. St. Paul saith, Eph. ii. 19. " Ye are no more strangers and foreigners, but fellow-citizens with the saints, and of the household of God."

When he exhorteth us to withdraw from all wicked affections, he calleth us to our Saviour Jesus Christ, who is our life, who is in heaven: must we not then take pains to come unto him? Now let us meditate upon this subject with solemnity, seeing we are to celebrate the Lord's Supper next sabbath. Let us see how we are disposed: for God will not have us come to him as liars and deceivers. Therefore, let us see if we are disposed to receive God, not as a guest that travelleth by the way, but as him that hath chosen us for his dwelling place forever: yea, as him that hath dedicated us to himself, as his temples; that we may be as a house built upon a rock. We must receive God by faith, and be made truly one with our Lord Jesus Christ, as I have already shown.

And are these things practised among us? Nay; on the contrary, we seem to despise God, and as it were, put Jesus Christ to flight, that he may no more be acquainted with us. Observe the disorder that is among us; should I enumerate the difficulties, where should I make an end? Let every one open his eyes! It is impossible for us to think of the confusion that reigns among us now-a-days, without being amazed, if we have any fear of God before us. Men flatter and please themselves in their sins, and have become as stocks and stones; so that in us is fulfilled that which was spoken by the prophet; namely, that we have a spirit of drunkenness, and a spirit of slumber, and can discern nothing.

As I have already observed, if we had any fear of God before our eyes, we should be cast down in ourselves, and not only be ashamed, but detest such confusion as is seen among us both in publick and private. We see men so far out of the way, that one would think they were disposed to lift up themselves against God, and do contrary to his will. Thus, it seemeth that the word of God serveth to harden men in wickedness; for they seem to be at defiance with him both in publick and private; as I have already observed. We daily hear blasphemies, perjuries, and other contempts of God's name: we see that there is disorder among us; that we are so far from honouring God, that many act as hypocrites, while others withdraw themselves from all order of the church, and are worse than the Turks and Heathens.

As for my part, I may say, that I am ashamed to preach the word of God among you; seeing there is so much confusion and disorder manifested. And could I have my wish, I would desire God to take me out of this world. We may boast that we have a reformation among us, and that the gospel is preached to us; but all this is against us, unless we attend to the duty which God hath enjoined upon us. It is long ago that God warned us, and it is to be feared he will speak no more in mercy, but will raise his mighty arm against us in judgment.

Therefore, let us take heed to ourselves; for these things are not spoken to stir us up against God, but that we may know our faults, and learn to be more and more displeased with ourselves, that we may not become hardened against God. For he calleth us to repentance, and showeth that he is ready to receive us to mercy, if we return and embrace the promises, and fear the threatenings, contained in his gospel. Those that are in publick office, ought to be diligent in their duty, that justice may not be violated. Those that are appointed ministers of the word, should have a zeal to purge out all filthiness and pollution from among the people.

We should so examine and cleanse ourselves, that when we receive the supper of our Lord Jesus Christ, we may be more and more confirmed in his grace; that we may be ingrafted into his body, and be truly made one with him; that all the promises we perceive in the gospel, may be better confirmed in us. We must know that he is our life, and that we live in him, as he dwelleth in us: and thus we know that God owneth and taketh us for his children. Therefore, we should be the more earnest to call upon him, and trust in his goodness, that he may so govern us by his holy spirit, that poor ignorant creatures may through our example be brought into the right way. For we see many at this day, who are in the way to destruction. May we attend to what God hath enjoined upon us, that he would be pleased to show his grace, not only to one city or a little handful of people, but that he would reign over all the world; that every one may serve and worship him in spirit and in truth.

SERMON IX.

2 Timothy, Chap. iii. *verses* 16 *and* 17.

16. All scripture is given by inspiration of God, and is profitable for doctrine, for reproof, for correction, for instruction in righteousness:
17. That the man of God may be perfect, thoroughly furnished unto all good works.

The word of God being called our spiritual sword, there is need of our being armed with it: for in this world the devil continually fighteth against us, endeavouring to deceive, and draw us into sin. Therefore, St. Paul saith, the word of God deserveth such reverence, that we ought to submit ourselves to it without gainsaying. He likewise informeth us what profit we receive from it; which is another reason why we should embrace it with reverence and obedience. There have been some fantastical men at all times, who would wish to bring the holy scripture into doubt; although they were ashamed to deny that the word of God ought to be received without contradiction. There have always been wicked men, who have frankly confessed that the word of God hath such a majesty in it, that all the world ought to bow before it; and yet they continue to blaspheme and speak evil against God.

Where is the word of God to be found, unless we see it in the law, and in the prophets, and in the gospel? There it is that God hath set forth his mind to us. To the end, therefore, that men may not excuse themselves, St. Paul plainly showeth us, that if we will do homage to God, and live in subjection to him, we must receive that which is contained in the law and the prophets. And that no man might take the liberty to choose what he pleaseth, and so obey God in part, he saith, the whole scripture hath this majesty of which he speaketh, and that it is all profitable. To be short, St. Paul informeth us, that we must not pick and cull the scripture to please our own fancy, but must receive the whole without exception. Thus we see what St. Paul's meaning is in this place; for when he speaketh of the holy scripture, he doth not mean that which he was then writing, neither that of the other apostles and evangelists, but the Old Testament.

Thus we perceive that his mind was, that the law and the prophets should always be preached in the church of Christ; for it is a doctrine that must, and will, remain forever. Therefore, those that would have the law laid aside, and never spoken of again, are not to be regarded. They have made it a common proverb in their synagogues and taverns, saying, " we need neither the law nor the prophets any more :" and this is as common a thing among them, as among the Turks.

But St. Paul bridleth the christian, and telleth us, that if we will prove our faith and obedience toward God, the law and the prophets must reign over us ; we must regulate our lives by them ; we must know that it is an abiding and an immortal truth ; not flitting nor changeable ; for God gave not a temporal doctrine to serve but for a season, for his mind was, that it should be in force in these days ; and that the world should sooner perish, and heaven and earth decay, than the authority thereof to fail. Thus we see St. Paul's meaning is, that we should suffer ourselves to be governed by the holy scripture, and seek for wisdom no where else.

We must observe, (as hath already been said,) that he giveth us no liberty to choose what we list, but he will have us to be obedient to God in all respects, approving what is contained in the holy scripture. Now let us notice the two points which are here set forth. He saith first, *All scripture is given by inspiration of God ;* and then addeth, *and is profitable.* These remarks St. Paul maketh upon the holy scripture, to induce us to love it, and to show that it is worthy to be received with great humility. When he saith it is given by the inspiration of God, it is to the end that no mortal man should endeavour to control his almighty power. Shall miserable creatures make war against God, and refuse to accept the holy scripture ? What is the cause of this ? It is not forged by men, (saith St. Paul,) there is no earthly thing in it.

Whosoever will not show himself a rebel against

God, and set him at nought, must submit himself to the holy scripture. St. Paul addeth in the second place, besides the reverence which we owe to God by doing him homage, we must confess, moreover, that he sought our profit and salvation, when it pleased him to teach us by the holy scripture : for he will not have us busy ourselves with unprofitable things. Therefore, if we be diligent in reading the holy scripture, we shall perceive that there is nothing contained in it, but what is good and fit for us, from which we may obtain some benefit.

How unthankful we are, if we accept not the blessings which God offereth so freely ! After St. Paul had magnified the holy scripture, showing that the majesty of God appeareth in it, he would also give us some taste, that we might come to it with an affection and desire to profit thereby ; knowing that it was God's design, and the end he aimed at. Let us always remember that the holy scripture will never be of any service to us, unless we be persuaded that God is the author of it. When we read Moses, or any of the prophets, as the history of mortal men, do we feel a liveliness of the spirit of God inflaming us ? No, no ; it is far from it.

Therefore the holy scripture will be lifeless, and without force, until we know it is God that speaketh in it, and thereby revealeth his will to man ; for St. Paul saith, *the holy scripture is given by inspiration of God.* The *pope* will boast, that all he hath put forth, is from God : thus we see, that by using the name of God for a cloak and covering, the world hath been deceived, and kept in ignorance from the beginning. For there never was any poison of false doctrine, but that it was put into a golden cup ; that is to say, was hid under this honourable title ; *that God spake to man.*

If we are content to be governed by the will of God, our faith will be rightly sealed ; so that we may perceive that it is not the illusion of satan, neither a fable invented by men; I mean those things contained in the holy scripture, which were spoken by God, who is the author of them. Let us consider the infinite goodness of our God, in that it hath pleased him to seal up his truth in our hearts, and cause us to feel the virtue of it; while unbelievers are left in their ignorance, to despise the authority of the holy scripture.

We may gather from what St. Paul saith, that there is no authority in the church of God, but what is received from him. If then we admit of a doctrine, it must not be borrowed from the authority or wisdom of men, but we must know that it came from God. This is a notable point; for God will prove thereby whether we be his people or not. He is our king indeed, because we have no laws nor ordinances except from him; our souls are not guided by chance, for he ruleth over us, and we are subject to his yoke. If this be not the case, we do not show that God governs us, though we make ever so formal pretensions; they are but false shows.

St. Paul doth not inform us, in order to prove the holy scripture to be an undoubted truth, that Moses was an excellent man; he doth not say that Isaiah was very eloquent; he declareth nothing of them whereby he may raise the credit of their persons; but he saith, they were instruments in the hands of God: their tongues were guided by the Holy Ghost: they spake nothing of their own, but it was God that spake by them. We must not consider them as uninspired men, but as servants of the living God; as faithful stewards of the treasures committed to them.

If these things had been observed, men would not have come into such horrible confusion, as the papists are at this day. For upon what is their faith grounded, except upon men? There is nothing but hypocrisy in all their doings. It is true, they declare God's name, but in the mean time observe their own ceremonies. But St. Paul requireth us to confine ourselves to the holy scripture; because God speaketh there, and not man. Thus we see, he excludeth all human authority: God must have the pre-eminence above all creatures whatsoever; they must submit themselves to him, and not presume to encroach upon his sovereignty. When we go into the pulpit, we ought to be assured that it is God that sent us, and that we bring the message which he committed to us.

Let him that speaketh, speak according to the word of God: that is, let him show that he doth not thrust himself in rashly, nor patch up with any of his own works, but that he holdeth forth the truth of God in its purity; he must make his doctrine edifying to the people, that God may be honoured thereby. Seeing the doctrine of men is here cast down, let us banish it from the church of Christ, that it may never be admitted again. Therefore, let us beware and keep ourselves steadfast in the simplicity of the gospel: for our Lord hath been so gracious, as to reveal his will to us by the law and the prophets: then let us hold fast that which we have received, and not suffer men to bind our consciences, and frame articles of faith for us according to their own notions.

St. Paul saith, *all scripture is profitable.* Therefore, if the holy scripture be profitable, we are very unthankful in not applying ourselves to the study of it. Who is there among us that doth not desire profit and salvation? And where can it be found, except in the holy scripture? Wo be unto us then, if we hear not the word of God, who seeketh nothing but our happiness. Moreover, we must not read the holy scripture in order to support our own notions, and favourite sentiments; but submit ourselves unto the doctrine contained therein, agreeably to the whole contents of it; for it is all profitable.

When I expound the holy scripture, I must always compass myself by it; that those who hear me, may be profited by the doctrine held forth, and receive edification thereby. If I have not this affection, if I do not edify those that hear me, I commit sacrilege, and profane the word of God. Those also who read the holy scripture, or come to hear the sermon, if they seek any foolish speculations, if they come hither to recreate themselves, they are guilty of profaning the gospel. If we divert the holy scripture from its proper use, and seek questions in it, without endeavouring to profit by it, we pollute it.

St. Paul hath taught us that we must come to God with earnest desires, seeing he seeketh nothing but our profit and salvation. He showeth us also that we must not pollute the holy scripture, to make it serve our own fancy; but knowing it is God's mind that it should be made profitable to us, we must come thither to be taught: yea, and taught in that which will be profitable for our salvation. Now it remaineth for us severally, to examine and see what this profit is: if St. Paul had pronounced but this one word, the sense might have been somewhat obscure: but he openeth it so plainly, that we cannot mistake his meaning; for he saith, "The scripture is profitable for doctrine, for reproof, for correction, for instruction in righteousness; that the man of God may be perfect, thoroughly furnished unto all good works."

St. Paul doth not set forth a single use of the holy scripture, but when he hath spoken of the doctrine, he addeth, *to reprove, correct, and instruct.* And why so? It is not enough for God to show us what is good, because we are so cold that we should hardly perceive it: therefore he must needs stir us up to an earnestness: we must know that he speaketh to us, and that we are bound to obey. Thus we see there is no dead doctrine in the holy scripture; but there are reproofs and corrections to stir us up, that we may come to God.

St. Paul saith, *all scripture is profitable for doctrine:* and then addeth, *to reprove, correct,* &c. Why beginneth he with this word *doctrine?* Because it is the natural order; for if we are not taught to say, this is the truth, exhortation will be of no use: therefore, we must first of all be made sensible, that that which is taught us, is good, and true, and right. Thus the word doctrine signifieth, that we must be instructed in the truth, that we must be thoroughly resolved in it, and so edified by it, that we doubt not its authenticity. St. Paul informeth us, that this doctrine is to know Jesus Christ, and put our whole trust in him; to live soberly, righteously, and godly.

When we call upon God by prayer and supplication, we must put our trust in him, and look to the heavenly life whereunto he calleth us: we must mortify all our wicked affections, and conform ourselves to his righteousness. The doctrine of the gospel, in few words, is this: to know God, and put our whole trust in him: and to know by what means he is our Saviour; namely, in the person of our Lord Jesus Christ, his only begotten Son, who died for our justification. This is the way whereby we are reconciled to God, and cleansed from all sin; from which proceedeth the confidence we have to call upon him, knowing that he will not cast us off, when we come in the name of him who is appointed our advocate.

When we consider that there is nothing but sin and wickedness in us, we must learn to be displeased with ourselves, and serve God fervently, with a pure heart: this is the doctrine contained in the holy scripture. We must understand the meaning of St. Paul, when he saith, *to reprove:* that is, if we would be well instructed in the school of God, we must confess ourselves guilty; we must be pricked to the heart; we must be reproved for our faults. When the word of God is rightly expounded, the faithful are not only edified, but if an unbeliever come into the church and hear the doctrine of God he is reproved and judged. By this we understand, that although the unbeliever may be wrapped in darkness, and pleased with his own ignorance, yet when God so enlighteneth him, that he seeth the misery and wickedness in which he hath lived, when he seeth his deplorable situation, while giving ear to the word of God, he perceiveth the heavens open, as it were, and that man was not made for this life only, but to be exalted to a higher station. Thus unbelievers are convicted.

And to make it more clear, St. Paul addeth, the secrets of the heart are then disclosed; for we know while the word of God is buried, no man taketh heed to himself; our hearts are in darkness. What then must we do? We must apply the word of God to our use, and be awakened out of sleep: we must no more forget God, nor the salvation of our own souls; we must search the very depth of our hearts, and examine our whole lives; that we may be ashamed of our filthiness, and become our own judges, to avoid the condemnation that is ready at the hand of God. Thus we understand what St. Paul meaneth by the word *reproof*.

It is not enough for men to lay the blessings of God before us, and say, this is God's will; but we must be awakened to think upon it in good earnest, and look narrowly to ourselves: yea, and to draw near to God, as if he had summoned us to appear before his judgement seat: we must bring all to light, that we may be ashamed of our evil deeds: and when we breathe into this heavenly air, we must be careful not to turn aside from the right way.

It is not enough to be thus *reproved,* but *correction* must be added likewise : we must be chastised, as it were, by the word of God; to the end we may be reformed. We must forsake our sins ; we must be sharply dealt with, that they may be plucked out by the roots, and separated from us. Thus, when we have been roused to think upon God, we feel condemned before him, while our sins are laid open to view ; and we become guilty in the sight of both God and man. Moreover, we must be drawn to it by force ; if we have been drunk with delicacies, if we have indulged ourselves in folly and vanity, and have thereby been deceived, the corrections must be quick and severe, that we may give God the honour, and suffer him to reform us, and bring us into subjection to his will.

When a father seeth his children conduct themselves improperly and viciously, he thinketh it not enough to say, why do you so ? but he will say, you wretched creatures, have I brought you up, and hitherto fostered you, to recompense me thus ? doth it become you to do me this dishonour after I have used you so gently ? you deserve to be given into the hands of the hangman. So it is with us : when God seeth that we are more rebellious against him than disobedient children are against earthly parents, hath he not occasion to be angry with us ? Not that there are any unruly passions in him, but he useth this earnestness that we may be brought into subjection, and learn to obey him.

Now we may judge whether it would be enough for a man, when he would expound the holy scripture, to discourse upon it as though it were a mere history; for if it were so, that which St. Paul saith concerning it, is unprofitable : it would be sufficient for him to have said, to preach the gospel, we need only say, *thus spake God.* The office of a good and faithful shepherd is not barely to expound the scripture, but he must use earnestness, and sharpness, to give force and virtue to the word of God. St. Paul saith in another place, that the shepherds of the church must be earnest, even to be importunate; and not only show the people what is good, but reprove them.

It is true, he saith it must be done meekly, mildly, and patiently: but however it be, corrections must be used. Men must not say, this is too hard to be borne, you must not deal after this sort; let those who cannot suffer reproof, seek another master beside God, for they are not worthy to hear his word. The world would gladly be spared; and we see many who are ready to burst with rage, when they are threatened and corrected. They say that they wish to be won by mildness. Then let them go to the devil's school; he will flatter, yea, and destroy them.

But as for the faithful, after they have received the doctrine, they must humble themselves, and be willing to receive reproof: they must be exhorted when they have done amiss: they must be reproved for their sins and offences, that they may be purged from all iniquity. In this manner we must behave ourselves, if we wish to be instructed in the doctrine of God. St. Paul addeth, *the scripture is profitable for instruction in righteousness; that the man of God may be perfect, thoroughly furnished unto all good works.* When he saith that the holy scripture is profitable to instruct in righteousness, he shutteth out whatsoever man might bring; showing that we shall not become righteous by observing the works introduced by man.

We see how the papists torment themselves in vain; observing whatsoever is enjoined upon them by men. In what consists their righteousness? upon what is it grounded? It is grounded upon this, *the church so commandeth.* But St. Paul showeth that there is neither religion nor doctrine, except in that which is contained in the holy scripture; yea, and in that only is righteousness. Do they then follow that which

God hath commanded? No; for they go entirely contrary to it. Therefore, if we wish to have our lives well framed, let us not ground ourselves upon the works of men, but let us follow that which God enjoins upon us.

If we regulate our lives by the instructions contained in the holy scripture, we shall be justified thereby: but the doctrine of men is but folly, and an abomination to God. Then let us remember it is not without cause that St. Paul saith, *to instruct in righteousness*. Again, he giveth us to understand, that to be good divines, we must live holy lives. The word of God is not given to teach us how to talk, to make us eloquent and subtle, but to reform our lives, that the world may know we are the servants of God. If we wish to know whether a man profiteth by the gospel or not, let us mark his life: men may know how to talk, they may make a fair profession of godliness, and yet not have their lives correspond with the written word of God.

St. Paul informeth us that we must make the word of God our counsellor, that we may walk uprightly, and form our lives by it: thus, *the man of God may be perfect, and furnished unto all good works*. In this manner we must be instructed in righteousness, and reject the inventions of men, for with them God is not well pleased. Men wish to serve God according to their own notions, and therefore bring their own works into the account; but God will not allow them. St. Paul, seeing such impudent boldness in men, that they cannot keep themselves within the bounds which God hath set them, points out the disease, that it may be healed: he saith, if we have the word of God in our hearts, we shall be upright in life, and furnished unto all good works.

Men may boast as much as they please, that their works are virtuous and holy; but when they shall appear before the heavenly judge, all will be as chaff.

When we mix our inventions with that which God hath commanded, we injure all: Therefore we may conclude, that whatever things are forged by men, are nothing but corruptions. The papists call these good works: to fast upon a saint's eve; to eat no flesh upon Friday; to keep Lent; to serve saints; to go from altar to altar, and from chapel to chapel, to attend mass; to go on pilgrimage, &c. they have forged so many laws and statutes, that a man cannot understand them. But we must at last appear before the great judge, to give an account of all our actions.

It is said here that we shall be furnished unto all good works, if we profit by the holy scripture. But what will become of the traditions and inventions of the papists? in which the word of God seemeth to be buried. They make not one hundredth part as much of the word of God, as they do of men's traditions. Therefore let us not deceive ourselves willingly, considering we shall have the measure of our perfection: God shutteth out whatsoever is added to the holy scripture, and showeth that it shall not be reckoned or received by him; therefore men make their items in vain; it will but double their condemnation.

A man might ask, of what use is the gospel, seeing there is so much uprightness in the law and the prophets? This may be easily answered; the gospel was not given to add any thing to the law or the prophets; let us read the New Testament; we shall not find one syllable added to either; it is only setting forth that which was taught before more plainly. It is true that God hath been more gracious to us, than to the fathers who lived before the coming of our Lord Jesus Christ; matters being more clearly set forth to us, although there is nothing added. So then, when St. Paul saith that we shall find uprightness and perfect righteousness in the law and in the prophets, it diminisheth not the gospel.

There is an agreement in all the holy scripture; of the *Old*, and *New* Testament. The doctrine which was contained in the law, has been expounded so familiarly to us by the apostles since Jesus Christ, that we cannot say we must do this or that, but we must confine ourselves to that which was commanded from the beginning. God hath made known his will in such clear terms, and hath given so many reasons why we should believe it, that we must be convinced of its truth, unless we are monsters in wickedness. Therefore, if we will profit by the holy scripture, we must study holiness of life, knowing that God will not be served after our own fancy; for he hath given us a certain rule whereby we should regulate our lives, and such a one as cannot be found fault with. Let us then direct our hearts, thoughts, and affections, to that which is contained in the holy scripture; and then the heavenly judge will receive us. We must be the more induced to attend to these things, because our good God draweth so nigh, and setteth forth his will in such a plain manner to us, that we cannot excuse ourselves, unless we cleave wholly to him.

SERMON X.

2 Timothy, Chap. ii. *verses* 20 *and* 21.

20. But in a great house there are not only vessels of gold and of silver, but also of wood and of earth; and some to honour, and some to dishonour.
21. If a man therefore purge himself from these, he shall be a vessel unto honour, sanctified, and meet for the master's use, and prepared unto every good work.

WHEN we see contemners of God, who set bad examples, we sometimes depart from the right way, thinking we have somewhat to excuse ourselves before God; not knowing that these should serve as an exercise of our faith. Therefore, St. Paul not only exhorteth us to separate ourselves from all iniquity, that we may not be like the contemners of God, but he exhorteth us not to be offended, nor take occasion to doubt, when we see men wickedly disposed. He hath before illustrated this matter, but now confirmeth it by a fit similitude. And first, that we may not think ourselves worthy of pardon if we do evil and follow those who despise God, St. Paul saith, *in a great house there are divers vessels.* If the cupboard or table be furnished with vessels of gold and silver, in the kitchen may be seen vessels of wood and stone. When we see such a variety, we marvel not at it; for if a man should cast his gold and silver among the refuse of his house, what should we think of him? Should we not say he was mad? If it is not improper to have vessels appointed to an unseemly use in a great house, shall we not be content with it in the house of God? Shall we allow greater privileges to mortal man than to the living God?

St. Paul exhorteth the children of God, though they be placed among the wicked, not to defile themselves with their wickedness; but rather be moved to a carefulness by this means, that they may shun evil examples and separate themselves from their company; that they may dedicate themselves the more diligently to God. Thus in few words we have the apostle's meaning. As we have already shown, the lesson given us here by St. Paul, is very profitable: for if there be wicked men and hypocrites in the church of God, who continue among us for a season, and are highly esteemed, it must not trouble us; for the house of God is great.

Some understand this to include all the world; and it might reasonably be taken so: however, of this we shall speak more at large hereafter. St. Paul had just made mention of backsliders, who fell away, after they had made a profession of their belief in the gospel. This matter bringeth us great comfort; seeing the church of God is spread throughout all the world, and many being called to the gospel. Let us put the case to those here assembled; are there not vessels of gold and silver enough to furnish a cupboard or table? and are there not likewise vessels of wood and earth, which, after they have served awhile, are to be cast away, or burnt, or no account made of them.

Although we might wish for nothing but purity in the church of God, for nothing that could be found fault with, yet notwithstanding, we must expect to see stumbling-blocks. And why so? Because God assembleth together a great variety of vessels. It is said, Mat. xiii. 47. that the church of God or kingdom of heaven is like unto a net that was cast into the sea, where all sorts of fishes were gathered; which, when it was full, was drawn ashore, and the good gathered into vessels, but the bad cast away: so it is when the gospel is preached; many will seem to receive it, yea, and for a season appear to be of the number of the faithful; but they soon turn aside and become separated from them.

The church of God is also compared to a floor, where wheat is mixed with chaff: but the floor is to be purged, the wheat gathered into the garner, and the chaff burnt with unquenchable fire. Mat. iii. 12. and Luke iii. 17. This is to show us, that during this life, the church of God shall never be without mixture. There always will be hypocrites, who will assent to the doctrine of faith; or at least will have a place in the church, and be taken for christians: but in the end it will be ascertained that they are not sons, therefore they will be disinherited. We have a figure of this in the case of Ishmael; who, for a season, was above Isaac; being the elder son: but he was cast out, and Abraham was constrained to cut him off: Gen. xxi. 14.

Before we go any farther, we must answer a doubt that might here be raised. It is said in the Psalms, that those who come into the mountain of God, and have a place to dwell in his temple, must be without blemish, and must walk uprightly. This, at first sight, seems to destroy the idea that there are vessels to dishonour; for all must be chosen to serve God, and must be sanctified to obedience. To what doth God call us but to holiness? Are we not vessels of his temple? Yea, are not every one of us a part of his sanctuary? Must we not be consecrated to him, and purified from all blemishes and pollutions? In the places which we have mentioned, we are taught what manner of persons those whom God calleth to himself ought to be: it is not said that all are such; for there are many who although they are commanded to dedicate themselves to God, remain filthy and wicked.

When it is said that those who have clean hands and pure hearts shall dwell in God's holy mountain, many will boast that they are his children, and that they are faithful, who are not worthy to be reckoned of his household: but in the end, they will be cast off. After they have occupied a place under this false title, and have wickedly abused the name of God, he will banish them, as we have already noticed concerning Ishmael. The wicked who dwell in the temple of God, seem to do well for a time, but they soon begin to despise their maker, and use deceit, malice, violence, extortion, and cruelty toward their neighbours. They may grow up in the church, but in the end, God will separate the goats from the sheep.

In the second place, St. Paul exhorteth us *to purge ourselves from all the filthiness of the wicked.* And why so? If we be partakers of their wickedness, God will be displeased with us. Therefore, if we wish to be honourable in his church, we must not only have this outward title before men, but we must live in obedience to his will, and show that it is not for nought that God hath chosen us to himself. Let us understand what is said in the text; that if there be wicked men mixed among the good, we may not be troubled beyond measure. We see some so nice, that if they can spy any fault in the church, or if the reformation is not so perfect, or such as might be wished for, they will cry out, how now! is this the church of God? and will separate themselves from it; thinking that they defile themselves, if they belong to a company that cannot wholly correct the faults of their own members.

We ought indeed to be earnest and zealous, and endeavour to put away stumbling-blocks: if we see evil in the church, it must be purged out; it must be cut off speedily, and not suffered to grow. We must all earnestly desire the temple of God to remain pure and clean: yet, notwithstanding, we must suffer many things to remain, which cannot be taken away; when we cannot remedy them, we must mourn. However the world may go, we ought not to estrange ourselves from the church of God, under the pretence that all men walk not as they ought. And why so? In a great house, if a man go into the kitchen, and see vessels that are worth nothing, or of which there is but little account made, he would not be angry; for they are appointed for the use of the kitchen, and thus serve for the cleanliness of the house. If a man should be so peevish as to forsake all, and say, I will never come into this house again, because I see vessels here that serve to no purpose, except to gather up the filth of the kitchen, would he not be ignorant? On the contrary, he may see that pains are taken to serve him the better.

Therefore, when we see such vessels in the church

of God, let us not be grieved, and take occasion thereby to withdraw ourselves from it, but let us still go on, and persevere. St. Paul meant to show us here, that although the wicked endeavour to bring the name of God into reproach and dishonour, they cease not to serve his glory. And how? God turneth their wickedness into goodness. When we look at the wicked, we think they were made to dishonour God, to destroy the reputation of his majesty, and abolish his justice; to turn all things upside down, that the world may have no more knowledge of him. This is what they aim at, and the devil pusheth them forward; but they cease not to be vessels: that is to say, God will find means to use them in such a manner, that he will be glorified by them. Not that this excuseth them, nor that they may cloak themselves with such a mantle, as though they served him, for this was not their mind or intention.

Let us submit ourselves to the providence of God; for if we be angry and peevish, and say all things are out of order, we shall not be excused. Let us be fully resolved, that in despite of satan, God will be glorified. Moreover, let us learn to practice this doctrine; namely, when we see nothing but blemishes among us, and that stumbling-blocks are not removed as they ought to be; when there is not so much honesty as is requisite, and men shut their eyes for fear of seeing the light; when they dissemble, and when there is not rigour and severity enough used to keep them in order, let us mourn, and, if possible, correct such irregularities.

We must not think because we see these disorders in the church of God, that it is utterly destroyed; that our Lord Jesus Christ is able to do no more; but rather consider that although the wicked disfigure the beauty of the church, although they defile and pollute it, yet notwithstanding, God will be glorified: after they shall have troubled the church long enough, God will bring them to their end, and show himself to be their judge. Therefore let us be patient, knowing that we have a wonder working God; who worketh by such means, that he causeth even the devil and wicked men to praise him. It is true that the devil will always show himself as much as possible a deadly enemy to God's glory, and will endeavour by all means in his power to tread it under foot; but after all, God turneth his wickedness into good. So fareth it with the wicked, who go about to bring all things into disorder, and to take the kingdom of God from among us, and raze out the remembrance of his name. But when they have done all they can, they still remain vessels.

St. Paul treats upon this subject more extensively in the ninth chapter to the Romans, where he plainly showeth that the reprobates and castaways, not only those who make profession of christianity, but they that are open enemies to the gospel, are God's instruments and vessels, whereby he causeth his glory to appear; although their intention is entirely different. He speaketh as much of those who denied God, and made no pretensions to be of his household, as of hypocrites, who made for a season some show. For example, there is a wicked man that seeketh to mix heaven and earth together, as it were; satan hath employed him this way and that, and it is thought for a time that he will do great wonders; but God showeth that the matter is in his hand, that he hath him bridled, and in subjection, and that he is his instrument.

It is true that the wicked are not led by the spirit of God to do evil; it would be blasphemy to say so; for the spirit of God leadeth us to justice and righteousness. Although the devil entice men into wickedness, yet notwithstanding, God ruleth over all; yea, and in such a manner that he applieth their wickedness to his service. Therefore, seeing it is so, let us learn to be patient. When there are stumbling-blocks in the church, we must not nurse the evil, (as I have previously shown,) but every one ought to be active, and endeavour as much as possible to cleanse the church from all manner of filth.

After we have done all in our power, if we are unable to make it better, let us wait patiently, while God useth the evil, and turneth it to a good end. Therefore, let us understand what is here taught us; namely, that the wicked are vessels; that is, they shall be constrained to serve God. They are not inclined to do good, but God can draw them by force, and dispose of them according to the counsel of his own will; which surpasseth our understanding. They serve in his house, not to honour; and yet the name of God ceaseth not to be glorified: it doth in no wise lessen his justice, wisdom, virtue, and goodness. Thus God keepeth all things in order, although the wicked are mixed among the righteous.

If a man therefore purge himself from these, he shall be a vessel unto honour. This is the second part of that which we have before noticed. When we see that the church of God is not so well reformed as might be wished, we are apt to think all is lost, and that God ruleth no more in the world. But St. Paul instructeth us not to be disconcerted, but wait patiently till it please God to turn the malice of the wicked to his own glory. If we be constant, and not shaken by the confusion in the world, the end will always be good. When we are among the wicked, we must not join with them in their wickedness, but separate ourselves from them. St. Paul exhorteth us to cleanse ourselves from those of whom he spake, and dedicate ourselves to God. It is a hard matter for a man to walk through mire and dirt without defiling himself; or to go into a foul and filthy place, and return without stain or spot upon him.

Therefore we must take heed, and be careful when

we are conversant with those who contemn God. When we are among lewd men and hypocrites, we must be circumspect in our conversation: for nothing is more easy than to become inwrapped in the pollutions of the world, and by them infected: for this reason St. Paul saith, let us beware. This admonition was not given for one time only, but it must be observed to the end of the world. Let us learn then, that although there ought to be some policy in the church to correct faults, to keep people in the fear of God, and induce them to live an honest life, yet we shall see many things that are hurtful, which will turn us out of the right way, unless we are watchful.

We may be joined with the wicked until we depart out of the world, but let us endeavour to cleanse ourselves from their filthiness; let us pray to God, that he would turn us from their pollutions, and purify us by his holy spirit; that his righteousness may always reign in our hearts. Thus we see the meaning of St. Paul, that we should cleanse ourselves from those of whom he spake: as if he had said, although we are conversant with the wicked, who would wish to lead us into their company, and have us partake of their wickedness, yet we cannot excuse ourselves if we become like them; for God did not sanctify us in vain, when it pleased him to choose us to himself.

St. Paul saith, we must cleanse ourselves: not that we are able to do it of ourselves, but because God will have us attend to his service. From the reading of this sentence, some have concluded that we can cause God to choose and predestinate us; but this is overthrowing the groundwork of our faith. It is gross beastliness to say, we must separate ourselves from the wicked if we will have God to choose us. For it is as much as if we should say, before we were born, before the world was made, it was necessary for us to prepare ourselves, that we might be worthy of God's adoption. This doctrine is so foolish, that it does not deserve particular notice. For he chose us before the foundation of the world was laid; he respected no deserts of ours whatever.

Again, there are others that would establish a free will; saying, we are commanded to cleanse ourselves, and therefore it must depend upon our own industry. But these men show themselves ignorant; and that they are not well informed in the holy scripture. For when God showeth us what our duty is, he doth not say that it is in our power, or that we are able to do it: but he exhorteth us to do that which is good; and worketh in us, because we are not able to perform it of ourselves. Therefore let us learn in this way to cleanse ourselves, that we may not be like the wicked.

God saith, Ezekiel xxxvi. 25. "Then will I sprinkle clean water upon you;" that is, the Holy Ghost. We are commanded to cleanse ourselves, but God showeth that this belongeth to him, and that it proceedeth from the pure grace of his holy spirit. Why then doth St. Paul use this language? Our nature moveth nothing at all; it is the Lord that worketh all the good that is in us; he giveth us the will, and also the strength and affection, that we may fight against wickedness: thus yielding and giving to us that which belongeth to himself. He worketh in us in such a manner, that it seemeth we do it ourselves.

The believer taketh great pains, and laboureth to purge himself from the filth of the world, that he may not be infected with the corruptions of the wicked. In this we fight manfully; but it is God that driveth us to it; it is he that giveth us virtue: in short, he giveth us the will, and enableth us to execute it, (as St. Paul saith,) all of his free goodness. That we may not be idle, we are thus exhorted in this place; and such exhortations are not needless. Having made some observations upon the words purging or cleansing ourselves, we shall notice the following clause of the same verse; namely; *he shall be a vessel unto honour, sanctified, and meet for the master's use, and prepared unto every good work.*

When he speaketh of vessels of honour, he showeth that it is not enough to have a place in the church of God, and bear the name of christians, but we must be separated from sin and uncleanness. It is true that all those who are baptized, all who are partakers of the supper of our Lord Jesus Christ, and joined with the faithful, are already separate from unbelievers: no man will say that they are Turks or Heathens. Yet notwithstanding, something more than this is necessary; we must not have the outward mark only, and boast of our baptism and profession to serve God, but our life must witness that we are indeed his children; that when we are governed by his holy spirit, it may be a witness to certify us of our adoption.

This is the meaning of St. Paul, when he saith, we must be vessels unto honour. And why so? It may be, although we are in the church of God, yea, and of those that are most forward, that in the end we shall be cast aside as a broken vessel, or forsaken as a vessel of wood, that serveth to no purpose: such is the end of hypocrites, who vaunt and boast that they are of the number and company of the children of God. They may indeed be vessels, and God may use them, but they are to dishonour; for he will bring them into confusion.

Therefore let us take heed, and see that we are vessels unto honour; not to have an outward or temporal mark only, that we may be taken for the children of God, but that we may be chosen for his everlasting inheritance; and by this means draw near to him. We must not only be vessels in the house, but of the temple; to serve to make holy sacrifices and oblations, that we may thereby serve and honour

God. When God maketh the malice of men serve his glory, (as it is said of Pharaoh,) it is like drawing fire out of water : it is so great a work that it is difficult to comprehend it.

We glorify God when we give ourselves wholly to his service, and seek nothing but the honour and glory of his name : and this is done when we act as true children, and labour both in body and soul to apply ourselves to his use. He not only saith that we are vessels of his temple, but that we are the priests that bear them. Thus God useth us as vessels of honour, dedicating both body and soul to his service : yea, he maketh us vessels to be applied to whatever shall serve for his holiness, that he may reign among us. Therefore we must take so much the more pains to sanctify ourselves; as it is said, Isa. lii. 11. "Be ye clean, that bear the vessels of the Lord." Again, we know how God hath commanded that the vessels should be kept clean and pure, and that no unclean thing should be put therein.

Therefore, seeing we are the vessels of the temple, the bearers and keepers of them, let us beware and dedicate ourselves to the use of God, which is honourable. Seeing we are his temples, each one of us, and all together, let us be careful to keep ourselves in all pureness. Seeing God doth us this honour to receive us as vessels of his temple, and dwelleth in us by his holy spirit, must we not be purged from all filthiness? God will not dwell in a filthy place, his house must be pure and holy : whatsoever cometh near him must be sanctified. We cannot be fit to serve God, unless we be vessels of honour; that is, given to all good works.

If we would serve God as he requireth, we must give ourselves to good works : that is, we must seek nothing but to obey his will, and answer his holy calling. Then we shall not only be instruments in his hand, but we shall be vessels of honour, governed by his holy spirit. Thus we shall close our remarks upon this text.

To make a short conclusion, let us learn not to disorder ourselves; though the devil cast many troubles in our way, though storms and tempests arise, though there be not so much regularity in the church as could be wished, yet let us still keep on our way, and not think that this lesseneth the majesty of God: for in a great house there must needs be *vessels of wood and of earth.* God will prove our affection; let us therefore be watchful, and think not to be excused, if we join the wicked in their pollutions. When the wicked rejoice and endeavour to mar our comfort, let us withdraw from them: when sin reigneth, and every one is endeavouring to draw his companion into destruction with him, let us run to our God, praying him to keep us under the governance of his holy spirit; and thus frame ourselves to the pureness spoken of by St. Paul.

Seeing we are insufficient for these things, that besides our weakness, there is nothing but corruption in us, let us pray God to send us his pure waters, spoken of in Ezekiel xxxvi. 25. that we may be cleansed from all our filthiness, and made fit subjects for his service. Then we shall desire to live in obedience to the will of God; yea, and that frankly, not by restraint and force. When God is glorified by the works of the wicked, (as he saith he hath kept them for his glory,) we must know that it is not their intention to worship him: but by a wonderful providence, he draweth good out of evil: even as he turned darkness into light when he made the world.

SERMON XI.

Titus, Chap. i. *verses* 7, 8, *and* 9.

7 For a bishop must be blameless, as the steward of God; not self-willed, not soon angry, not given to wine, no striker, not given to filthy lucre;
8 But a lover of hospitality, a lover of good men, sober, just, holy, temperate;
9 Holding fast the faithful word as he hath been taught, that he may be able by sound doctrine both to exhort and to convince the gainsayers.

Those who are called to preach the word of God, may here learn what their office or duty is; and thereby be enabled to perform it faithfully to God, and to the church. This subject must be well understood, if we wish to profit by the text. Christians, generally, ought to understand what is requisite in a good minister. They ought not to choose him thoughtlessly, or from mere fancy and ambition; but they should have the profit and common salvation of all the children of God before their eyes. This ought to be observed by those who are already in the office; and unless they conduct themselves according to the direction of the Holy Ghost, they ought not to be suffered to continue therein.

The virtues here spoken of by St. Paul, are necessary for all ministers of the word of God; who must show the way to others: it is also a useful lesson for us all. The minister ought to behave himself well, in a godly manner; and the people ought to refrain from all kinds of wickedness. The minister must point out the way, and set good examples; and the whole body of the church regulate their lives according to what is here taught them. We see from St. Paul's writings, in the verses preceding the text, that those whom he called *elders*, he now calleth *bishops;* which signifieth watchmen or overseers. He giveth this name to all who are called to preach the word of God.

Therefore, it was corruption and abuse in the Popish Church, to call one man alone chief bishop: for that was changing the speech of the Holy Ghost. Thus we see that Satan laboureth to turn us from the pure simplicity of the word of God. And besides, it is wrong for a man to separate himself from the order which hath been established by the authority of God. All therefore whom God calleth to preach his word, must be well grounded in the truth; and must be faithful watchmen. It is said, Ezekiel iii. 17. Son of man, I have made thee a watchman unto the house of Israel: therefore hear the word at my mouth, and give them warning from me."

The title which is given to all shepherds, showeth plainly what it is that God calleth them to do: they are to watch and take care of the flock, while other men sleep. They cannot serve God, only by employing themselves to serve his people. The greatest honour that ministers of the word of God can have, is to be diligent and faithful in the church. St. Paul saith, it is reasonable that the watchmen or bishops should be without blame; seeing they are governours in the house of God. We may notice what he said to Timothy; how he exhorted him to beware and take heed, that he might know how to behave himself in the house of God, over which he was placed as ruler: he therefore saw the necessity of Timothy's walking uprightly.

Is it a small matter to be a minister of God, and governour of his house? St. Paul showeth in this place, that those to whom God hath committed his word, and called to preach the gospel, ought to conduct themselves in an exemplary manner. God honoureth us in a marvellous manner, when he calleth us into his house, and admitteth us as members of his family; where he will dwell among us, and nourish and protect us. Therefore, when we are sensible that we are not separated from our God, that our belief is well grounded, that he hath gathered us into his flock upon the condition that he will be with us to the end of the world, we ought to be moved to love him more earnestly, and serve him better.

The church is called the house of God, that we may magnify the inestimable goodness of our Creator, who hath been pleased to draw near and make his abode therein: he hath assembled us together, and joined us to himself, that he might take care of our salvation; that he might be our master and overseer; not for his own profit, but for our salvation. This text is not only for the ministers of the word, but it should profit all the faithful; we should all apply it to ourselves, for our own instruction.

St. Paul saith, *a good shepherd must be blameless; not self-willed, not soon angry, not given to wine, no striker, not given to filthy lucre:* as if he had said, the man that is given to these vices, doth nothing but infect the place he is in, and injure the church. He that is blemished with any of these faults, is not a fit man to serve God: these things must therefore be purged out from among us. The first virtues required by St. Paul, in order to qualify a man to preach the word of God, is to abstain from the faults which are here condemned.

As it is the duty of a faithful minister to draw those home that are gone astray, so it is likewise his duty to endeavour to keep those in peace and unity who are already in the church. If he be stubborn and self-willed, he will offend the flock of God, and make a breach in the church. In order, therefore, that he may serve God, and keep the church in peace and concord, he must not trust too much to his own understanding, nor be obstinate in his own opinion.

When we teach others, we must be willing to be taught also. For if we are not willing to learn, that others may profit by our instruction, we shall never be able to do our duty. Therefore, he whom God hath placed as teacher in his house, must show himself ready and willing to receive doctrine, and good instruction. We must be ready to hearken when other men give counsel, and be willing to receive information. Thus we have the meaning of St. Paul in few words: namely; those who are called to preach the word of God, must take heed that they be not self-willed, but willing to be taught: they must be meek and quiet spirited; not puffed up with pride, but endeavouring to edify others; they must not think that they know all things, but on the contrary desire to learn continually, and be gentle in their behaviour. Those who are lofty spirited, and self-willed, often become schismaticks: that is to say, they trouble the church of God, and divide it into sects.

It is not without cause that St. Paul correcteth this haughtiness: for we see by experience that it is a great evil. *The minister must not be soon angry:* this fault is much like the other. For if a man doth not govern himself in this respect, it will be a great hinderance to him in serving God. *Not given to wine;* because drunkenness increaseth this haughtiness, and is, as it were, a kind of madness. The minister of God must therefore be sober: for if drunkenness reign in him, he will be destitute of reason, equity, and modesty. Thus we see what a number of deadly plagues are here enumerated, of which the ministers of the word of God must beware.

They must be *no strikers* nor brawlers: they must not be like soldiers or contentious men, who are always ready to fight and wrangle; this fault must be corrected also: neither must they be *given to filthy lucre;* they must not be covetous. The minister that seeketh to enrich himself by his office, will not do his duty faithfully. He will put a gloss upon the word of God, and endeavour to please and gratify man : to be short, he will disguise or falsify every part of it; or he will endeavour to ascertain in what way he can make it most advantageous to himself. Therefore, if covetousness reign in ministers of the word, they will undoubtedly prove to be false teachers; whose chief study will be to pervert good doctrine, and turn the truth into a lie.

Those who do their duty faithfully, must edify the church of God, and abstain from all crimes and faults that are notorious. They must be *lovers of hospitality*. They must be kind toward strangers, and receive them courteously. This should be observed at all times; but in the days of St. Paul there was a particular reason why it should be observed; for the poor christians were as birds upon the boughs; they were constrained to take their flight from place to place, according as persecutions were raised against them; yea, they were oftentimes compelled to hazard their own lives. We see therefore that great compassion was needful. Thus we see it is not without reason that the holy apostle requireth the bishop, who ought to be as a father to the church, to be liberal and kind to strangers, and to receive them courteously.

They who are called to preach the word of God, must be *lovers of good men*. This virtue is similar to the one last mentioned. They must be courteous and affectionate to those in necessity, and endeavour to relieve their wants. Those who are destitute of pity, who are content to live at their ease, and never look at the condition of others, will never show any compassion toward their fellow-creatures, nor entertain those that are persecuted and afflicted. For this cause St. Paul placeth these two virtues together.

We shall next notice the words which follow: namely; *sober, just, holy, temperate*. *Soberness* referreth to a man's life. *Justice* is upright dealing; whereby a man should take care that every one hath his proper due; and be willing to suffer himself, rather than wrong others in any way whatever: this is what St. Paul meant by the word justice. *Holiness* consisteth principally in obedience to God: that is, we must do no harm to our neighbours, but live chastely, devoting ourselves entirely to the service of God; we must attend strictly to prayer and supplication; we must withdraw ourselves from the world, and not be given to vanity; we must not lead a dissolute life, but live in humbleness and submission to the will of God: this is the holiness here spoken of.

Temperance comprehendeth whatever might be understood by the word Soberness. It is not enough to be temperate in meat and drink, but there must be modesty and honesty in all the rest of our lives: our hands, our eyes, our ears, and our mouths, must be bridled. This is what St. Paul meant by temperance. As if he had said, we must be settled and established: we must have no improper dealings; no vain, lewd, or dissolute actions; but we must live in obedience to the will of God, that men may know we have renounced the world.

Holding fast the faithful word as he hath been taught. This is the principal thing required in ministers of the gospel. They must not only be instructed that they may teach others, but they must be strong in the faith, and maintain the doctrine of the truth, that it may remain safe and sound. If we have taken fast hold of the truth, it shall never escape us; although the devil labour to make us shake it off, yet shall we never be turned aside. We must exhort with wholesome doctrine, and reprove those that speak against it: that we may be able, and have the means to teach those who are willing to obey God; and that we may have virtue to fight against those that speak against the truth, against enemies of the word of God, against rebels, against contemners, against men who go about to make confusion and disturbance in the church, that they may go away with shame.

St. Paul showeth us that the shepherds must point out the way to all the faithful. Why should the ministers of the word of God be sober, just, and holy? Why should they be modest, not given to wine, nor to strife and blows? Why should they be settled and established in the truth? To the end the word of God may not be spoken of with irreverence; and that they prove their doctrine by a godly life, and so ratify it, that it may be received more readily: and likewise that the people may follow their examples, and endeavour to imitate all those virtues which they see in their shepherds.

The meaning of St. Paul was not confined to ministers only, when he exhorted them to beware of intemperance, covetousness, and pride, and be courteous, just, sober, chaste, &c. : but by their example, he exhorted all christians to behave themselves in such a manner, that soberness, justice, holiness, modesty, and all the virtues here spoken of, may be common among them. If we wish to be the children of God, let us correct the faults which are here condemned by St. Paul; and endeavour to follow the virtues which he hath recommended.

Although the minister may be governour in the house of God, yet notwithstanding, every member hath an office to fill. When God calleth some few to preach his word, he doth not forsake the rest, but will use every one, without exception, in his service. This is the condition, this the end, why God hath appointed us to preach the gospel; that we may devote ourselves to his service. When he conferreth this honour upon us, to receive us into his house, and adopt us for his children, it is not that we should be idle, but that he may hold us under his yoke, and cause every one of us to glorify him, that we may not be unprofitable: for it is not in vain that God hath called us to such an estate, and to so high a dignity, as to be of the company and fellowship of his children.

The ministers of the gospel must therefore look well to themselves, and likewise every member of the church must observe the rules here laid down, which are for the instruction of all, from the greatest to the least. Let us therefore be modest, sober, just, and holy; and so live that sin may no more reign among us. When men become drunkards, they not only blot out the image of God, but they become as dogs and swine. If we wish then to be taken for the children of God, must we not shun this vice? St. Paul excludeth all drunkards; he will not have us associate, or even be conversant with them; that they may be ashamed, and amend their lives: much less ought they to be admitted to the table of our Lord Jesus Christ.

Is not pride and loftiness contrary to the spirit of meekness, which is the true mark of the child of God? Whereby shall the world perceive that we have profited in the school of our Lord Jesus Christ, if we be not humble, meek, and lowly? Therefore, when haughtiness reigneth in a man, it is a token that he never was taught in the school of God. It is evident that the virtues here spoken of by St. Paul, ought not to be confined to ministers only, but they ought to be practised by the whole church. Much may be said of covetousness; for we plainly see that by thinking too much of this world, we forget the spiritual blessings, and the inheritance whereunto we are called. What will become of us, if covetousness reign in us, and we become so attached to the things of this world, that we think no more of the kingdom of heaven? Although we are daily reminded of this sin, yet notwithstanding, we are so prepossessed with earthly cares, and so bound to the world, that we cannot lift our minds on high to behold the heavenly life. Thus we see, that " where our treasure is, there will our heart be also."

Those that are given to the things of this world, have their minds and affections so placed upon them, that they cannot aspire to the heavenly inheritance whereunto we are called. Thus we see that covetousness is a deadly plague; it so blindeth men, that it depriveth them of that which God hath promised. It is not without cause that St. Paul saith, 1 Tim. vi. 10. "The love of money is the root of all evil." This love of money, or covetousness, carrieth with it wicked practices, deceits, treasons, unfaithfulness, and cruelty: in short, there is no wickedness but what proceedeth from covetousness. The covetous man forgetteth all uprightness in dealing; he will do whatever he desireth; he will spoil and rob; and in all his actions there will be wrong and injury; yea, and being without fear and reverence, he will openly mock God. Covetousness carrieth men so far, that they even murder one another. To be short, covetousness is a kind of madness that operateth upon men in such a manner, that they become devils.

This evil must not only be shunned by the ministers of the gospel, but every christian must avoid it. Moreover, it is said that the children of God must be peace-makers. It is a mark whereby our Lord Jesus Christ will have them known. Christ saith, Mat. v. 9. " Blessed are the peace-makers; for they shall be called the children of God." Now if we be given to revenge and strife, if we be lovers of quarrels, do we not show that we are destitute of the love of God?

We must always endeavour to be courteous toward strangers, when we see them in a destitute situation; for this has been observed even among the heathens. When we see the church of God tormented by tyrants and enemies of the truth, we must entertain the poor christians who are banished from their country: if we do not, is it not a token that we renounce God? It is the will of God that we should be strangers in this world; yea, and we are his children upon this condition; as it is said, Heb. xi. 9. God is in heaven, and yet he cometh down hither, and governeth us: thus he giveth an example, that we may know what pity we ought to have upon those that flee to us, and claim refuge; who are as sheep scattered by ravenous wolves.

St. Paul therefore spake not only to the ministers of the word of God, but in their persons, he gave, as it were, a looking-glass, by which all may regulate their lives. If we are so rigorous that we will not help those who are in want and necessity, nor be moved with compassion when we see our neighbours suffer, it is certain that the love of God is not in us. If it is not our duty to help one another, it would have been necessary for God to have made as many worlds as there are men; that every one might devote all his attention to himself. But he hath made us fellow-workers: we must not conclude that each one is born for himself, and liveth in this world merely for his own profit; but we must do good to our neighbours, and endeavour to serve them: and wo be to us, if we be not thus minded.

We must be good natured, and do all the good we possibly can to our fellow-creatures; we must help those that have need of help; we must relieve the needy, and use our goods for the benefit of those in distress: yea, and we must do it with a frank and liberal heart. If we have not this love and good will toward our neighbours, it is an evidence that we are not God's children. If we mistake in judging upon these points, we go contrary to the dictates of nature itself; though we were without faith and religion, and without any knowledge of the law and gospel.

If men are intemperate in eating and drinking, they are also dissolute in their whole life : will they therefore say that they are nourished at the hand of God ? Even the heathens have more honesty, (as we have before mentioned,) who are taught by nature. We ought always to remember when we eat and drink, that every blessing is received from our Maker. If we abuse these blessings by becoming gluttons and drunkards, is it not an evidence that we have forgot heaven, and have become attached to the things of this world ? When St. Paul saith, the bishops must be just and holy, we must remember that the admonition extendeth to every one of us : we must all live honestly and uprightly, rendering to every man his just due. Let us therefore endeavour to govern ourselves in such a manner, that the world may see there is true holiness in us : let us implore God to separate us from all the pollutions of this world, that we may be brought up in his house, and governed by his holy spirit.

It is evident that the rule here given by St. Paul, concerneth all the faithful ; and that no one ought to think himself exempt therefrom. It now remaineth for us to know how we may become partakers of these virtues, and how we may tame and abolish such faults as are here condemned. Alas ! it cannot be done by our free will, nor by our own ability : but God must work in us. And how ? We must be members of our Lord Jesus Christ. It is said, we must be sober, just, holy, temperate ; and how shall we become so ? When the Holy Ghost shall rule in us, then shall we have these virtues. It is said we must flee drunkenness, intemperance, strife, debate, and pride. And how ? By having the spirit of meekness, the spirit of humbleness, the spirit of wisdom and discretion, and the spirit of the fear of God : all which was given to our Lord Jesus Christ, that he might make those that believe in him partakers of it.

Therefore, seeing we are by nature intemperate, full of vanity, lies, ambition, and pride, given to unrighteousness, deceit, and robbery, let us come and submit ourselves to him who is appointed our head; knowing there is no other way for us to be kept in obedience to God, and to live according to his will, only to be united to our Lord Jesus Christ : for then are we strengthened by the outpouring of the Holy Ghost, which is the fountain of all holiness, of all righteousness, and of all perfection. This is the way whereby we must come to that which is here commanded by St. Paul : and this is the cause why we are called to the communion of our Lord Jesus Christ.

When the apostle defineth the gospel, and the use of it, he saith, we are called to be partakers of our Lord Jesus Christ, and to be made one with him ; to dwell in him, and he in us ; and that we be joined together by an inseparable bond. This being the case, we are greatly confirmed in the doctrine by the holy supper. When we come to this holy table, we must know that our Lord Jesus Christ presenteth himself, to confirm us in the unity which we have already received by the faith of the gospel, that we may be grafted into his body in such a manner, that he will dwell in us and we in him. We must therefore take pains, and endeavour to profit by this holy union more and more, that we may cleave more closely to the Son of God.

Thus we may see the holy supper is very requisite : and we keep it often, because we are earthly and fleshly while living in this world, and have need to be often reminded of that which was once taught us. Let us beware that we profane not the grace which God thus bestoweth upon us, when he maketh manifest by such a sign, that we are indeed partakers of his Son; but let us pray him to govern us by his holy spirit in such a manner, that when we come to his holy table, we may not pollute it.

We must consider that we are poor miserable creatures, and must come to our Lord Jesus Christ to be cleansed from all our filthiness; for he is the fountain of all pureness. We must be purged from all our sins, and so ruled by the holy spirit, that the world may perceive we are united to him, and drawn from temporal to spiritual things. May we so fight against the vanities of our flesh, and all wicked affections, that we seek nothing but to fashion ourselves more and more to the image of our God, and to be owned as children and heirs of the heavenly inheritance.

SERMON XII.

Titus, Chap. i. *verses* 10, 11, *and* 12.

10 For there are many unruly and vain talkers and deceivers, specially they of the circumcision;
11 Whose mouths must be stopped, who subvert whole houses, teaching things which they ought not, for filthy lucre's sake.
12 One of themselves, even a prophet of their own, said, The Cretians are always liars, evil beasts, slow bellies.

St. Paul saith, *there are many unruly and vain talkers and deceivers*, in the towns and country of Crete. He maketh mention of this to Titus, who was then in that island, that he might be careful in appointing men to govern the church, who would reprove those that rose up against the truth of God, and endeavoured to trouble the church. As dangers and necessities increase, men ought to provide remedies. So, when we see wicked men strive to bring confusion into the church, we must be careful and zealous, and endeavour to keep all things in their proper order. St. Paul informeth us that there were many rebels even among the faithful, and such as attempted to preach the gospel, who were given to vain prattling and filthy lucre; teaching that which did not edify.

When we see the church of God so troubled by the wicked, it is the duty of ministers to strive to keep things in a proper condition: they must be armed, (not with a material sword,) but with the word of God, with wisdom and virtue, that they may be enabled to resist the ungodly. When we see so many turn from the right way, let us be careful, and endeavour to have the church of God provided with good rulers, that Satan raise not up stumbling-blocks among us. When St. Paul speaketh of these vain deceivers, he mentioneth the Jews in particular; who were the flower of the church, the first born of the house of God. We know that the Gentiles were as wild branches, which God of his grace grafted into the stock of Abraham. Although we see that the Jews were anciently the true heirs of salvation, and that the inheritance of life belonged to them, yet notwithstanding, St. Paul notes them as being the greatest disturbers of the church.

When the wicked sow tares, (whether it be of false doctrine or wicked talk,) to turn the faithful from the right way, if we dissemble, or make as though we saw them not, the weak will become infected, and many will be deceived; thus there will be a general plague: but if we point out such men, they will be shunned, and therefore will do but little evil. When we see men who do nothing but pull down, and endeavour to cause trouble in the church, we must labour to bring them into the right way: but if they remain steadfast in their wickedness, we must make them known; we must disclose their filthiness, that men may abhor them, and separate themselves from their company.

Shall we leave the church of God among thieves and wolves, as it were, and let the whole flock be scattered, and the blood of our Lord Jesus Christ trodden under foot? Shall we suffer all order to be abolished, the souls which have been redeemed destroyed, and in the mean time shut our eyes and be silent? If we act thus, are we not cowards? Let us therefore endeavour to bring back those that have strayed, who are not utterly past hope: especially if their faults be secret: but when they fall into such wickedness as to make confusion in the church, we must use a different remedy; we must show them what they are, and hold them up to the view of the world, that they may be avoided; we must not spare them, because the whole salvation of the people of God is in danger.

We must not be moved by favour toward the person of any one, and say, "this man is worthy of commendation; he is yet to be regenerated:" we must not think so much upon those men who seem honourable and privileged at the present day, as upon our duty. We have already shown that the gospel came from the Jews; that they were the holy root, the chosen people, the church of God. Therefore, when they had such prerogatives, might they not have expected some privileges? It is evident, that by this they were enabled to do the more evil. They need not use this goodly title, only to say, "we are the first born of the house of God;" but they might say, "we are the people whom God hath chosen to himself; we are the stock of Abraham, who were adopted from all ages; we are they to whom God revealed himself; and it is through our means that you have the doctrine of salvation at this day." When they made use of such sayings as these, were it not enough to astonish the minds of the weak?

Let us therefore remember, that when persons of honour and dignity have been in credit a long time, and then become deceivers, and endeavour to sow tares and destroy the building of God, we must withstand them the more courageously; for they are far more dangerous than those of lower rank. If an ignorant man, who is but little known, be wicked, and disposed to do evil, he cannot pour out his poison afar off, for he is, as it were, fettered. But he that is of reputation and intelligence, who setteth himself on high that he may be seen afar off, who can boast of his credit, &c. that man, I say, will be armed like a madman; and if he be suffered, he may do much hurt.

Let us mark well when we see men that are honourable, whether it be on account of the office they fill, or the reputation they have had for a long time. In other places where St. Paul speaketh of those that pervert the truth of the gospel, and put forth errours and false doctrine, he calleth them hereticks: but in this place he calleth them *unruly and vain talkers and deceivers*, who will not be ruled by truth or reason. There are no worse enemies than traitors; who, under colour of God's name, come and make divisions in the church, and endeavour to destroy that which God hath established. We see some who will not say at first, that the doctrine which we preach is false; for they would be ashamed to speak in this manner, were they ever so impudent: but they will labour to bring the people into a dislike of it; this we frequently see. I would to God we were entirely rid of such infection and filth.

If these vain talkers and deceivers be let alone, if we take no notice of them, what will become of the church? Will not the devil win all? And shall we not be guilty of betraying the flock, and of destroying that which was built up in God's name? We must therefore consider that we have to fight not only against the Papists and Turks, who utterly reject the doctrine that we preach, but against home enemies; who go about maliciously and traitorously to bring to nought those things which are well devised and established, that Jesus Christ may not reign in full power; who endeavour to corrupt the word, that in the end, the sincerity of religion may be destroyed.

We ought to withstand such enemies courageously; but we are so far from it, that every one seemeth to thirst after nothing so much, as to be wittingly poisoned. If we doubted the purity of any meat, we should quickly abstain from it; for the love and care of this frail life leadeth us to it. But when God telleth us that it is poison to turn aside from his word, from the reverence we ought to bear him, and from the zeal with which we ought to be inflamed, we make no account of it. Some care for nothing but to hear vain curiosities; others have a longing to see the servants of God vexed, and this doctrine troubled, that they may triumph at it: thus they join hands with hereticks, as we have frequent examples. But the faithful must be put in mind of that which God teacheth them: if they wish to stand safe and sound, they must be watchful, and shun false doctrine. Yea, and when they perceive that Satan goeth about secretly, endeavouring to corrupt the word of God, which is preached to them, it is the duty of every one to employ himself, and be faithful, that he may withstand the temptations of the adversary: for St. Paul spake not only to Titus, but to the people generally.

Now let us observe what is added; *they subvert whole houses.* If one man only were misled by them, it would be too much; for men's souls ought to be precious to us, seeing our Lord Jesus Christ hath esteemed them so highly, that he spared not his own life, but freely gave it for our salvation and redemption. But when we shall see whole houses subverted, that is, every one without exception, it is far more detestable. When St. Paul spake of the horrible crimes of deceivers, he mentioned vain babbling and foolish imaginations ; he spake also of certain traditions which the Jews brought out of their law, of which they had a wrong understanding. Are we not then sufficiently warned? If we be turned from the right way, whom shall we blame for it? If Satan be suffered to deceive us, and we be given over to a reprobate state, it is no more than we deserve; because we have not used the remedy which God hath provided for us.

After St. Paul hath thus spoken, he addeth, it is *for filthy lucre's sake.* We therefore see, that as soon as we are carried away with covetousness, seeking after the goods of this world, it is impossible for us to preach the gospel in its purity. St. Paul saith that he preached the gospel in its purity, and held it forth in simplicity. Let all those therefore that teach the church, follow the example of the apostle : let them take heed to themselves, knowing that if they will serve God purely, they must be content with what he hath given them, and cast off all desire of riches. They must come to this conclusion, that they are rich enough, if they are enabled to edify the church of God : if the Lord causeth their labour to become profitable, they must be content therewith. This is what St. Paul meant to set forth in this place. The island of Crete, which at present is called Candia, formerly contained about one hundred cities or towns. St. Paul informeth us that the nation had indulged themselves in wickedness for a long time, and therefore have an evil name. He saith, " One of themselves, even a prophet of their own, said,

The Cretians are always liars, evil beasts, slow bellies."

Such reproaches as these, seem to take away all their reputation. Some imagine that St. Paul here showeth himself to be their enemy: for he writeth to Titus, not secretly, but that his letter might be read and published, that the Cretians might know what he said concerning them. Notwithstanding his rebukes, he had the pastoral charge of them. Thus we may learn, that although a man may desire the salvation of a people, and love them sincerely, yet he will not cease to point out the faults of which they are guilty: and indeed we cannot show that we love those whom God hath committed to our charge, unless we labour to correct the faults and diseases wherewith we see them infected. A good shepherd, therefore, though he rebuke the people sharply, must love them better than his own life.

It being the duty of those who are called to preach the word of God, to use plainness, and point out the errours of the faithful, they must not be offended or grieved when they are told of their faults. Many at this day think the gospel is not well preached, unless they are flattered: that is, they think men do not preach the word of God, unless they cover their sins, and endeavour to please them: but we here see another kind of divinity. Ministers, when they see any kind of wickedness among those who are committed to their charge, must not conceal it; it must be made known. It is better to put those to shame, who have been negligent and sleepy, than to hoodwink them, that they may become more blind.

The surgeon, who hath a wound to heal, cutteth away all the rotten flesh, or if there be any apostume, he purgeth it to the quick, to take away all the infection and corruption; so must the ministers of the word of God do, if they wish to discharge their duty faithfully toward those committed to their care : and those of the faithful must bear such correction patiently, knowing that it is necessary that they should be thus handled. They must not murmur against those who seek their salvation; for what shall it profit us to be honourable in the eyes of the world, if in the mean time God abhorreth us? But there are many who are displeased if they are told of their faults. If he who hath authority to teach, point out the wickedness that reigneth among them, they will be displeased with him, and mock him.

We see how justice is corrupted, and what favours are granted; men speak of wickedness in their houses, in their shops, in the streets, and in the market-place; but if it be mentioned in the pulpit, if wickedness be made known by the preaching of the word of God, we see them displeased, and full of malice. There is no man but what can say, "such a sin is common; such a man hath done such a fault." Every one may see what sins reign among the people; and yet, those who are appointed to watch over them, dare not reprove them, although their office requireth it of them.

It is said the word of God is like a two edged sword, which pierceth the most secret thoughts, separating joint and marrow : yea, it reacheth even to the bottom of the heart, and maketh known whatever sins lurk within us. If we wish to be taken for christians, we must have quiet and contented minds, and not be angry when we are reproved for our faults. When we have any apostume about us, we must be willing to have it lanced; when the sore is ripe and raging, let us be willing to receive the remedy, knowing it is for our profit. It is said by our Lord Jesus Christ, that he will send the Comforter; "And when he is come, he will reprove the world of sin, and of righteousness, and of judgement." Therefore, if we will not bow down our necks, and receive God's yoke, that is to say, if we do not condemn ourselves, and suffer him to exercise spiritual jurisdiction over us, by those whom he hath appointed to preach his word, we shall be condemned. This is the cause why the papists speak evil of us. St. Paul exhorteth us to walk uprightly, and to have a good conscience before God.

If we wish not to be condemned by infidels, we must be meek and patient, and show ourselves ready and willing to receive instruction from the word of the Lord. When our faults are made known to us, we must confess them. We are commanded throughout the scripture to reprove the wicked: but it is a common practice in these times for men to cast off all correction, and take free liberty in all manner of sin and iniquity, being under no subjection. But those who wish to pass for christians, must not behave themselves in this manner. St. Paul saith, "Admonish one another;" and again, "Reprove sin." To whom doth the Holy Ghost speak in these two places? To all the faithful without exception. For although God hath chosen some, to whom he hath given a special charge to admonish, exhort, and reprove those that do amiss, yet notwithstanding, he chargeth every man to set himself against sin and wickedness.

If this be lawful for those who have no public charge, what must the minister do, whom God hath expressly charged to fill this office? There are bastard christians among us at this day, who know not God, nor obey his word; therefore they will not bear correction. St. Paul reproveth the Cretians by putting them in mind of the witness of their own prophet; who saith, "The Cretians are always liars, evil beasts," &c. When God maketh known our faults, and reproveth us, he doth it for our salvation; we ought therefore to be displeased with ourselves, and confess our sins with the deepest humility. We gain nothing by being stubborn : it is of no use ; for if we will not bow, God will break us in pieces.

It seemeth that God wrought a miracle, in sending the gospel into Crete. Although the people were very wicked, yet notwithstanding, the Lord in his goodness visited them. We may therefore perceive that God hath no regard to our worthiness, when he calleth us to be first in his church; but he oftentimes does it to set forth the brightness of his mercy. If, when we were cast away, he reached out his hand and took us to himself, he deserveth so much the more honour and praise.

We have deserved nothing at his hands ; and if we have received the gospel, it is not by reason of our own virtue ; for nothing can move God to call men to himself, and make them know his will, but his free mercy. Let us therefore learn to glorify our God in the spirit of humility ; and if he hath chosen us, and forsaken others, and we wish to remain in possession of so great a blessing, let us examine our lives daily. When we see that there is nothing in us but wretchedness, and that we can do nothing but provoke him to anger, let us prevent his wrath by condemning ourselves. When every man judgeth himself, then shall we be justified before God ; who will not only purge us from all our wretchedness, but cause his glory to shine more and more, that we may have occasion to call upon him as our Father, and proclaim to the world that he hath redeemed us by the merits of his Son, that we may become his inheritance.

SERMON XIII.

1 Timothy, Chap. ii. *verse* 8.

8 I will therefore that men pray every where, lifting up holy hands, without wrath and doubting.

After St. Paul hath informed us that our Lord Jesus Christ came into the world, and gave himself a ransom for all, and that the message of salvation is carried in his name to all people, both small and great, he exhorteth every one to call upon God. For this is the true fruit of faith, to know that God is our Father, and to be moved by his love. The way is open for us to run to him, and it is easy to pray to him when we are convinced that his eyes are upon us, and that he is ready to help us in all our necessities.

Until God hath called us, we cannot come to him without too much impudent boldness. Is it not rashness for mortal man to presume to address himself to God? Therefore we must wait till God calleth us, which he also doth by his word. He promiseth to be our Saviour, and showeth that he will always be ready to receive us. He doth not tarry till we come to seek him, but he offereth himself, and exhorteth us to pray to him; yea, and therein proveth our faith.

St. Paul saith, Romans x. 14. "How shall they call on him in whom they have not believed? and how shall they believe in him of whom they have not heard? and how shall they hear without a preacher?" Thus it may be understood, that God is ready to receive us, although we be not worthy: when we once know his will, we may come to him with boldness, because he maketh himself familiar to us. The apostle addeth, Romans xv. " Praise the Lord, all ye Gentiles; and laud him, all ye people:"

giving us to understand thereby, that the gospel belongeth to the Gentiles as well as the Jews, and that every mouth ought to be open to call upon God for help.

We must call upon God in all places, seeing we are received into his flock. The Gentiles were strangers to all the promises which God had made to his people Israel. But the apostle saith, behold, God hath gathered you into his flock: he hath sent you his only begotten Son, even for the fatherly love which he bare you: you may therefore boldly call upon him, for it is to this end, and for this purpose, that he hath given you this witness of his good will.

As often as the goodness of God is witnessed by us, and his grace promised, (although we be wretched sinners,) as oft also as we hear that our sins were forgiven us by the death and suffering of our Lord Jesus Christ, and that atonement was made for our transgressions and the obligations which were against us, and that God is at peace with us, the way is opened for us to pray to him and implore his blessings.

It is said in Hosea ii. "I will say to them which were not my people, Thou art my people, and they shall say, Thou art my God." Therefore, as soon as our Lord God maketh us taste his goodness, and promiseth that even as he sent his only begotten Son into the world, he will accept us in his name, let us doubt not, but come immediately to him in prayer and supplication. If we have faith, we must show it by calling upon God. If we make no account of prayer, it is a sure sign that we are infidels; notwithstanding we may make great pretence to a belief in the gospel. Thus we see what great blessings God bestoweth upon us, when we can have the privilege of prayer.

God informeth us that if we call upon him, it shall not be in vain; we shall not be deceived in our expectations if we come to him aright; we shall never be cast off, if we keep in the way which St. Paul hath marked out; namely, if we have Jesus Christ for our mediator, and trust in the merits of his death and passion, knowing that it is his office to keep us. And as he hath made reconciliation between God and us, he will keep us through his grace and mercy, if we put our trust in him.

When we are made sensible of the blessings which God hath bestowed upon us, in granting us the privilege of calling upon him by prayer, we must exercise ourselves in this duty faithfully: we must be careful both morning and evening to call upon God, for we have need of his assistance every hour. Again; we cannot pray to God unless we have the spirit of adoption; that is, unless we be assured that he taketh us for his children, and giveth us witness thereof by his gospel. As oft therefore as we read in holy writ, *pray to God, praise him,* &c. we must know that the fruit of our faith is set forth by these words; because God hath revealed himself to us, and hath made the way easy whereby we may come to him.

I will therefore that men pray every where: we see also in the first epistle to the Corinthians, that the apostle saluteth all the faithful who call upon God, *both theirs and ours:* chap. i. 2. Here he joineth the Gentiles with the Jews; as if he had said, I will not confine the church of God to one particular people. It was so under the law, but after the wall was broken down, and the enmity between the Jews and Gentiles taken away, there was liberty among all nations and people, of calling upon God; because his grace is common to both Jew and Gentile.

Moreover, St. Paul meant to show that the ceremonies of the law were not to be continued after Jesus Christ was made manifest to the world. For in the time of the law, men were constrained to come together at the temple, to call upon God. It is true that the Jews prayed, every man at his own house, but it was not lawful to offer a solemn sacrifice except in the temple; for that was the place that God had chosen. According to the grossness of the people, it was requisite to have sacrifices, until the truth should be declared more plainly. The temple was a sign, which represents that we must come to God in one way only; and what is that? through our Lord Jesus Christ.

We cannot come nigh to God, unless we have one to lead us; we must therefore trust in him through the merits of Jesus Christ. The Jews had this in a figure; we have it in substance and in truth. Again; God thought proper to hold them as little children in the unity of faith, by means which were suitable for their rudeness; but at present we have such a clearness in the gospel, that we need those old shadows no more. Seeing that the order which God had established under the law is now abolished, that is to say, the order of the temple of Jerusalem, and all the rest of the ceremonies; we must stay ourselves no more upon them.

Our Lord Jesus Christ said to the woman of Samaria, John iv. 21. 23. " The hour cometh, when ye shall neither in this mountain, nor yet at Jerusalem, worship the Father. But the hour cometh, and now is, when the true worshippers shall worship the Father in spirit and in truth." In those days there was a great controversy between the Jews and the Samaritans; the temple of Samaria being built in despite of the Jews. Those that worshipped at the temple of Samaria, claimed the example of Abraham, of Isaac, and of Jacob. The Jews had the word of God. Christ saith, that in times past, the Jews knew what they worshipped, for they were ruled by a doctrine which was certain; but that the Samaritans were idolaters. But now, (saith he,) you must strive no more for the temple of Jerusalem, or for the temple of Samaria: and why so? because God shall be called upon in spirit and in truth throughout all the world.

Jesus Christ having made his appearance, the old shadows of the law are taken away; let us content ourselves therefore, seeing we have a temple which is not material, nor visible: yea, all the fulness of the Godhead dwelleth in our Lord Jesus Christ. It is sufficient for us, that he reacheth out his hand, being ready to present us before God: and that through his means we have an entrance into the true spiritual sanctuary, that God receiveth us, that the veil of the temple is rent, that we may no more worship afar off in the court of the temple, but may come and cry with open mouth, *Abba, Father.*

Abba, was a customary word, used in the Hebrew tongue; that is, in the Syrian tongue. St. Paul putteth two words, *Abba, Father,* in Hebrew and Greek, to show us that every man in his own tongue hath now liberty to call upon God. Yea, there is no more a particular place where we must come to worship: but as the gospel hath been preached throughout all the world, we must show that at this day every man may call upon God, and *pray every where, lifting up holy hands, without wrath and doubting.*

It is true, we may now have temples for our convenience, but not in such a manner as the Jews had them: that is, we are not under the necessity of coming to some particular place in order to be heard of God. If there were other places as convenient for us as this, there would be no difference between them. Let us therefore learn that all ceremonies ended at the coming of Christ. This is very necessary to be understood, in order to draw us from the superstitious notions of the papists, which only darken prayer.

The Jews had their lights, perfumes, incense, &c.;

and they had their priests of the law; by which we may understand, that we have need of a mediator between God and man. The papists keep all those things still; and in so doing, it is as much as if they renounced Jesus Christ. It pleased God to be served in shadows, (as St. Paul showeth, Col. ii.) before the coming of Jesus Christ, who is the true body; that is, the substance of all. Do not those that seek such ceremonies, estrange themselves from Christ? Do they not know that when Christ was here in the world, and took our flesh upon him, and suffered and died, that it was for this purpose, that we might put our trust in him, and have no more of these childish figures, which served only for a season? Thus, the papists, with all the fooleries which they use, not only darken the glory of our Lord Jesus Christ, but utterly deface it.

Let us therefore learn to worship God, and call upon him out of a pure heart; without all these mixtures, and things devised by our own brains; yea, and without borrowing that from the old law, which is no longer proper for us. We now have a full revelation in the gospel: let us not, therefore, do this injury to God, to put away the brightness which he hath caused to shine before our eyes; seeing the Son of justice, that is to say, our Lord Jesus Christ, is now made manifest to us. Why should we talk any more of walking in dark shadows, which were only of use when we were far from that great brightness which afterwards appeared?

We must pray to God as he hath commanded us in the gospel. The papists make pilgrimages, and go trotting up and down, this way and that, to find God: but in so doing they forsake him, and withdraw themselves wholly from him. Let us not follow these examples, but be confirmed in the doctrine of the gospel, wherein we are exhorted to pray daily, not doubting but God will hear us in all our requests.

When we make our prayers to God, we must not bring thither our melancholy or fretful passions, as though we would be at defiance with him, as one that prayeth when he is angry, or murmuring, being disquieted by reason of affliction which God sendeth, for in so doing we dishonour him.

There are some who make a show, as though they prayed to God, by protesting against him, because they are not dealt with according to their own fancy. Thus, they will come to God, but it is to be at defiance with him, as if a woman should ask something of her husband, and at the same time say, *Oh, you care not for me!* This is the manner of prayer which some use, but it would be better for them not to pray at all, than to come to God with a heart so envenomed with wrath. Let us learn therefore to pray to God with a peaceable heart. St. Paul showeth us, that besides diligence in our prayers, we must also join thanksgiving: and if we do not immediately receive what we desire, wait patiently, and be content until God be pleased to grant our requests.

So, then, we must pray to God without murmuring, without fretting or foaming, yea, without using any reply, to ask him why he suffereth us to languish. It appears that St. Paul had another meaning in this place; for he regarded the circumstance which we have mentioned before; to wit, that the Jews would gladly have shut out the Gentiles. For, say they, we are the children of God, he hath chosen us; and shall not the stock of Abraham have more privileges than the uncircumcised nations? The Gentiles, on the other side, mocked the Jews, and considered them as children, not knowing that the ceremonies of the law were at an end.

Thus, the Jews despised the Gentiles, and disdained them, and would not receive them into their company. The Gentiles, on the other hand, mocked the Jews for their rudeness, because they continued to hold fast the rudiments of the law. Here arose many schisms; one party setting themselves against the other; and the church was, as it were, torn in pieces; yet above all things, God commendeth unity and brotherly love. Let us examine the form of prayer given us by our Lord Jesus Christ: *Our Father which art in heaven,* &c. He doth not say, that every one, when he calleth upon God, shall say, *my Father!* therefore, when I say, "*Our*," I speak in the name of all; and every man must say the same.

We shall not have access to God by prayer, unless we be joined together; for he that separateth himself from his neighbours, shutteth his own mouth, so that he cannot pray to God as our Lord Jesus Christ hath commanded. To be short, we must agree together, and be bound in a bond of peace, before we can come nigh, and present ourselves to God. These discords and debates of which we have spoken, existed between the Jews and Gentiles. St. Paul showeth that they cannot call upon God, without being refused and cast back, until they be at peace one with another. This is the reason why he requesteth them here, to *lift up holy hands, without wrath and doubting.*

Thus the apostle advised them, not to enter into debates and contentions one with another. The Jews must not advance themselves above the Gentiles, because they were called first; nor the Gentiles condemn the Jews for the grossness of their understanding: all these contentions must cease, and a perfect reconciliation must be made, to show that they all have the spirit of adoption; that is to say, that they are governed by the spirit of God, even that spirit which bringeth peace and unity. Let us understand this doctrine: that before we can dispose ourselves to pray aright, we must have this brotherly love which God commandeth, and this unity and nearness.

He would not have each one to remain by himself, but would have us unite in peace and concord : although every one speak, though every one be apart in his own place, and pray to God in secret, yet must our consent come to heaven, and we must all say with one affection, and in truth, *Our Father.* This word *Our,* must bind us together, and so make us in fellowship one with another, that there will be, as it were, but one voice, one heart, and one spirit. Moreover, when we pray, let the churches be joined together. If we wish to pray aright, we must not do like those who endeavour to divide that which God hath joined together, under colour of some little ceremony which is not worthy of our notice, separating ourselves one from another, and dismembering the body; for those that conduct themselves in this manner, show plainly that they are possessed with the spirit of Satan, and are endeavouring to destroy the union that exists among the children of God.

Therefore let all controversy be laid aside, and trodden under foot; and let us in liberty and with freedom pray to God, being assured that our Lord Jesus Christ hath manifested himself to us, and that through his merits we shall obtain favour in the sight of God the Father. Truly, we cannot join with those that separate themselves from us : for example, the papists call themselves christians; and cannot we communicate with them in prayer ? No ; because they have forsaken Christ Jesus. We know that if we swerve from him the least jot, we get out of the way : therefore, seeing the papists have separated themselves from Jesus Christ, the distance is too great between them and us, to be joined together. But we must give our hand to all those that will submit themselves to Jesus Christ; and with mutual accord come and render ourselves up to God.

Our Lord Jesus Christ saith, Mat. v. 23 and 24. "If thou bring thy gift to the altar, and there rememberest that thy brother hath aught against thee, leave there thy gift before the altar, and go thy way: first be reconciled to thy brother, and then come and offer thy gift." Do we wish God to be merciful to us? If we do, we must lay aside all enmity one against another: for if we be divided among ourselves, God will cast us off; for he will receive none but those that are members of his Son. We cannot be members of Jesus Christ, unless we be governed by his spirit: which is the spirit of peace and unity, as we have already shown. Let us therefore learn to live in friendship and brotherly love, if we wish to be received when we come to God.

When we see any thing that may hinder our prayers, we must remember that the devil goeth about to put stumbling-blocks in our way; let us therefore shun them as most deadly plagues. There are many who seek nothing else, but to raise difficulties and disputations; as though the word of God was made to separate us one from another. We have already mentioned that the true intent of the gospel is, to call us to God; that we may be joined together, and made one in our prayers and requests to him. Those that indulge in contentious debates, and endeavour to advance themselves one above another, pervert good doctrine, and fight against it; and endeavour to bring the glory of God to nought. Therefore, they must not think that God will hear them when they pray to him, seeing they have not this unity and concord to go to him in the name of our Lord Jesus Christ.

St. Paul saith, *lifting up holy hands.* By this he would have us understand, that we must not abuse God's name, by coming to him in our filthiness; but that we must be purged and made clean : for prayer is called a sacrifice ; and we know that in the time of the law, when they sacrificed, they first washed themselves. And why so? Our Lord meant thereby to show us that we are full of filthiness, unclean, and not worthy to come to him, until we have been cleansed. But the figures of the law are now at an end ; we must therefore come to Christ, for he is our true washing. Yet notwithstanding, we must not continue in filthiness, for Christ Jesus was given that he might renew us by his holy spirit, and that we might forsake our wicked lusts.

God doth not command us to bring our filthiness and infections before him, but we must pray to him, acknowledging ourselves utterly confounded and ashamed, full of uncleanness and filthiness, ready to be cast off, unless cleansed through the merits of the Lord Jesus Christ. Thus, by acknowledging our faults and blemishes, we must run to this fountain, where we may be washed : that is, Christ having shed his blood to wash away our sins, we shall be accounted pure before God, and wholly clean. When Jesus Christ gave us the spirit of sanctification, although there was nothing but infection in us, he cleansed us from our faults, and gave us free access to God. Therefore, the apostle saith we must pray, *lifting up holy hands.*

In the time of the law and the Old Testament, God entertained the people with this ceremony, that he would have them purified before they offered sacrifice ; yea, before they made solemn profession of their faith in the temple. These things are not in use at present, among the christians, but we must keep the substance. And what is the substance? It is this ; although we have no visible water for cleansing, yet we must come to the blood of our Lord Jesus Christ, which is our spiritual washing. Sometimes the Holy Ghost is represented as *clean water :*

as it is said in Ezekiel xxxvi. 25. "Then will I sprinkle clean water upon you, and ye shall be clean; from all your filthiness, and from all your idols, I will cleanse you." This promise referreth to the coming of Jesus Christ. So then, God showeth us that instead of the old figures which he gave to the Jews, and instead of material and corruptible water, we shall be purified and made clean by the holy spirit.

David saith, Psalm xxvi. 6. "I will wash mine hands in innocency : so will I compass thine altar, O Lord." When David speaketh thus, he hath respect to the figures of the law. We shall understand this more easily, by noticing the passage where God reproacheth the Jews by his prophet Isaiah, because they came into the temple with filthy hands. It is said, Isa. i. "When ye come to appear before me, who hath required this at your hand, to tread my courts? Bring no more vain oblations: incense is an abomination unto me ; the new moons and sabbaths, the calling of assemblies, I cannot away with: it is iniquity, even the solemn meeting. Your new moons, and your appointed feasts, my soul hateth: they are a trouble unto me ; I am weary to bear them. And when ye spread forth your hands, I will hide mine eyes from you ; yea, when ye make many prayers, I will not hear: your hands are full of blood. Wash you, make you clean ; put away the evil of your doings from before mine eyes: cease to do evil."

As our Lord God reproved the Jews for coming before him with filthy or bloody hands, so he commandeth us by the mouth of St. Paul, to *lift up holy hands:* that is, not to be inwrapped in our evil affections. Thus we see what St. Paul meant ; seeing we have this privilege, that we may pray to God, and draw near to him as our Father, we must not think that he will hear us, if we come to him in our natural state of filthiness; for he will not hold those guiltless that take his name in vain. On the contrary, seeing Jesus Christ hath come to purge us, and make us partakers of the Holy Ghost, we must endeavour to become pure; and as we cannot do it ourselves, we must have recourse to our Lord Jesus Christ, who is the fountain of all pureness, and the source of perfection.

We must not pray to God, as though he were an idol, and required to be served in a worldly manner; but our minds must be raised above our earthly affections: and as we lift up our hands, so must our hearts be lifted on high by faith. As oft then as we have our hands lifted up toward heaven, so oft should our minds be led to God in consideration of our weakness: knowing that we cannot have access to him, unless we lift ourselves above the world: that is, unless we withdraw ourselves from unruly passions, and vain affections. When we say, *Our Father which art in heaven*, we are reminded that we must seek him there, and must climb up thither by faith, though we still dwell on earth.

Let us learn therefore to renounce every thing which God doth not allow, knowing that our salvation is in him alone. Let us put our whole trust in him, believing that he will aid and assist us in all our troubles and afflictions: for if we do not pray in faith, although the ceremony may be good of itself, yet shall it be vain and superfluous. Those who lift up their hands to heaven, and at the same time remain fastened to things on earth, condemn themselves; yea, as much as though they should set down their condemnation in writing, and ratify it by their own hand and seal; condemning themselves as hypocrites, liars, and forsworn persons. For they come before God, protesting that they seek him, and at the same time remain attached to things below. They say they put their trust in him, and at the same time trust in themselves or some other creature : they pretend to be lifted up to heaven by faith, and at the same time are drowned in earthly pleasures.

Let us therefore learn, when we pray to God, to be void of all earthly cares and wicked affections; knowing that there are many things which hinder us from coming to God. When we lift up our hands to heaven, it must be for the purpose of seeking God by faith ; which we cannot do, unless we withdraw ourselves from the cares and wicked affections of the flesh.

Now let us fall down before the face of our good God, confessing our faults, and praying him to put them out of his remembrance, that we may be received by him ; and in the mean time, that he would strengthen us, and sanctify us from day to day by his holy spirit, until we wholly cast off all our imperfections and sins : but as this cannot be done so long as we live in this mortal life, that he would bear with our infirmities, until he hath utterly put them away. And thus let us all say : Almighty God our heavenly Father, &c.

SERMON XIV.

1 TIMOTHY, Chap. ii. *verses* 5 *and* 6.

5 For there is one God, and one mediator between God and men, the man Christ Jesus ;
6 Who gave himself a ransom for all to be testified in due time.

AT all times and seasons, the world hath been so far from God, that all people have deserved banishment from his kingdom. Thus we see, in the time of the law, he chose a certain people, and gathered them to himself; leaving the rest of the world in confusion. Although men were so separated from God, yet do they all naturally belong to him ; and as he made them all, so doth he govern and maintain them by his virtue and goodness. Therefore, when we see men going to destruction, God not having been so gracious as to join them with us in the faith of the gospel, we must pity them, and endeavour to bring them into the right way.

St. Paul saith, *For there is one God :* as if he had said, God hath made all mankind, and hath them under his protection ; therefore it cannot be but that there is some brotherhood existing between us. It is true, that those who do not agree with us in faith, are at a great distance from us ; yet the order of nature showeth us that we must not utterly cast them off, but take all the pains we can to bring them again to the unity of the body ; because they are, as it were, cut off. When we see men thus scattered, well may we be astonished, when we reflect that we are all of the self same nature ; the image of God was imprinted in them, as well as in us. Moreover, that which should have been the strongest band to hold us together, hath caused the division, and made us enemies ; namely, the service of God, the religion of Jesus Christ.

Therefore, when we see poor unbelievers wander and go astray from the way of salvation, we must have pity upon them, and do all we can to reclaim them ; keeping in remembrance the words of the apostle ; *there is one God :* St. Paul addeth, *and one mediator between God and men.* Whereby he giveth us to understand, that our Lord Jesus Christ came not to reconcile a few individuals only, to God the Father, but to extend his grace over all the world. We see set forth through the whole scripture, that he suffered not for the sins which were committed in Judea only, but for those which were committed throughout the world.

The office of our Lord Jesus Christ was to make an atonement for the sins of the world ; and to be a *mediator between God and men.* Having taken upon him our flesh, and so far abased himself as to become man, we should submit ourselves to him, in all his requirements. Our Lord Jesus Christ was made like unto us, and suffered death, that he might become an advocate and mediator between God and us, and open a way whereby we may come to God. Those who do not endeavour to bring their neighbours and unbelievers to the way of salvation, plainly show that they make no account of God's honour, and that they try to diminish the mighty power of his empire, and set him bounds, that he may not rule and govern all the world: they likewise darken the virtue and death of our Lord Jesus Christ, and lessen the dignity given him by the Father.

The apostle, in his epistle to the Hebrews, saith, chap. ii. 17, 18. " Wherefore in all things it behooved him to be made like unto his brethren, that he might be a merciful and faithful High Priest in things pertaining to God, to make reconciliation for the sins of the people. For in that he himself hath suffered, being tempted, he is able to succour them that are tempted." If a man know not what adversity meaneth, he hath no compassion on those that suffer; but being drunk with pleasure, thinketh poverty to be nothing. Our Lord Jesus Christ was partaker of all our miseries, and tasted all our afflictions; sin only excepted. And why so? To the end, that when we come to him, he may be ready to help us; having tasted our afflictions in his own person, he entreateth God to have pity upon us.

When he appeareth as mediator, we have nothing to fear: we may come with uplifted hands, calling upon God our heavenly Father, doubting not but that he will receive us as his children, through the merits of his Son, and make us feel the fruit of our adoption: so that we may come familiarly to him, laying open our necessities, and making known the grief which tormenteth us, that we may be relieved therefrom. The papists endeavour to prove that the Saints are our patrons, and that they make intercession for us; alleging that we are not worthy to appear before God. But if this be the case, of what use is the office of our Lord Jesus Christ, who is mediator, and man?

Let us notice what is contained in the law: when God commanded the people to pray to him, he forthwith showed them in what manner they should perform this service; which was this: the people were to stand afar off in the court of the temple; neither the king nor any other one, except the *priest*, was allowed to approach the sanctuary; for he was the figure of our Lord Jesus Christ. This was the reason why he was clothed in new garments, and was consecrated and dedicated to God. The *high priest*, entering into the sanctuary, carried with him the blood of the sacrifice which he had offered; by which we may understand, that no man can find favour with God, only by virtue of the sacrifice which is offered in the person of our Lord Jesus Christ.

Thus, God hath shown by this solemn ceremony, that we could not call upon him, unless there were an advocate to make intercession for the whole body of the church; and that this intercession must be grounded upon a sacrifice offered. This is the reason why St. Paul, after he had spoken of the intercession of Jesus Christ, addeth, *Who gave himself a ransom for all.* For these things cannot be separated one from the other; the death and passion of the Son of God, and that he is our mediator, to the end that we may have access in his name to God the Father.

Hath not Jesus Christ appeared to show the truth, the substance, and the perfection of the figures of the law? and yet Satan striveth to darken our minds, that we may not perceive this mediator that was given. We see in the beginning of the gospel that there were many hereticks, who believed the angels to be advocates. St. Paul, speaking of such, saith, Col. ii. 18. "Let no man beguile you of your reward in a voluntary humility and worshipping of angels, intruding into those things which he hath not seen, vainly puffed up by his fleshly mind." St. Paul giveth such honour to Jesus Christ, that all other intercessours and advocates must give way, and he be received as the only Saviour.

For forty years past, a man might as soon have heard Mahomet called the Saviour of the world, as the Son of God named as a mediator and advocate among the papists. And at this day, if any of us call Jesus Christ a mediator and advocate, they will immediately commence quarrelling with us, wishing to know whether we mean that Christ is the only advocate, or that the Saints are advocates likewise. If we endeavour to maintain the dignity of the Son of God, they are displeased with us : let us therefore be armed with the doctrine of the apostle, which teacheth us that we cannot come nigh to God, only through the mediation of Jesus Christ.

The papists are so impudent, and past shame, (I mean their doctors,) that when they wish to prove the matter which they have forged against the pure doctrine of the gospel, they say, "it is true that there is a mediator, but he is not the only one : for when we call a man one, it is not understood that he only is in the world, and none else !" But is not that which St. Paul saith in this place, that there is *one mediator*, as true as that where he saith, *there is one God?* It is the just vengeance of God, seeing they have endeavoured to take away the office of mediatorship, that they should be brought into shame and ignominy : because they have dishonoured the Son of God, the Lord of glory ; him to whom the

Father commandeth both great and small to do homage; before whom all knees must bow, and in whose person we must worship the majesty of our God.

The papists acknowledge Jesus Christ to be the only mediator of redemption; that it is he alone that redeemed the world: but as touching intercession, that he is not alone, that the Saints who are dead have this office as well as he. The apostle saith, that we were redeemed by the blood of the Son of God, therefore we must pray for all the world; for there is one mediator that hath opened the way whereby we may come to God. Jesus Christ is not only called mediator because he hath made reconciliation by his death, but because he appeareth now before the majesty of God, that we through him may be heard; as St. Paul showeth in the 8th chapter to the Romans: Jesus Christ hath therefore redeemed us by his death and passion, and now maketh intercession for us before God.

When we are exhorted to pray one for another, it is not diminishing the office of our Lord Jesus Christ, but that through his means we may all be made one together. When a man prayeth for himself, he ought also to include in his prayers the whole body of the church; that we may not separate that which God hath joined together. The doctrine of the gospel must be our rule and guide: doth that lead us to departed Saints? doth it appoint them for our patrons and advocates? No, no: there is not a syllable in holy writ that maketh mention of it. It is true, that while we live in this world, there ought to be mutual charity between us, and every one ought to pray for his neighbours; but if I do any thing more than the scripture directeth me, I go astray.

In the law it was said, that the people should not come near the sanctuary, but should tarry in the court; and that no man should enter into it, but him that offered the sacrifice. Even so let us consider our own unworthiness; knowing that we are not only earthly creatures, but that we are full of sin, having become polluted and unclean in Adam; therefore we can bring nothing to recommend us to God, because we are not worthy to open our mouths before him : let us then acknowledge our disease, that we may come to the remedy. And what is this remedy? It is to have our Lord Jesus Christ for our High Priest; he who shed his blood, *and gave himself a ransom for all.* Therefore, let us not doubt but that God is now merciful to us, seeing Christ hath reconciled us to him, by virtue of his death and passion.

As the High Priest bore the names of the children of Israel upon his shoulders, and had before him a tablet which contained twelve precious stones, signifying the twelve tribes of Israel, even so Jesus Christ bore our sins and iniquities upon the cross, and now beareth us, as it were, in his heart : this is the foundation upon which we stand. Therefore, let us not doubt but that we shall find favour with God, if we come to him in the name of this mediator. We must not devise advocates and patrons after our own notions, but content ourselves with the simplicity of holy writ. Jesus Christ is called the mediator, not only because he maketh intercession for us at present, but because he suffered for the sins of the world.

Therefore, let us learn to glorify God, and thank him with all humbleness, because it hath pleased him to draw us out of the abominations of the papists, that we may be stirred up to walk in fear and carefulness. Seeing it hath pleased God to give us such an advocate and mediator as his own Son, let us not be afraid to come and present ourselves before him, and call upon him in all our necessities : not that each one must do so privately, for himself alone, but let us all pray to God for the whole body of the church, and for all mankind,

When we pray to God, our prayers must be sanctified and consecrated by the blood of our Lord Jesus Christ. We have no need of the sprinkling of the *pope's* holy water; but the price of which St. Paul speaketh, must make satisfaction for us before God. We may rest assured that God will not cast away the sacrifice, whereby he hath become reconciled to us, but will be content therewith. When we pray, if we do not ground ourselves upon the death and passion of our Lord Jesus Christ, we must needs be in doubt and perplexity; and thus all our prayers will be vain and unprofitable. The scripture informeth us, that if we do not pray in faith, we shall not be profited thereby.

Who gave himself a ransom for all: when the apostle speaketh thus of our Lord Jesus Christ, he abaseth whatsoever men might presume upon, relative to their own satisfactions, as they term them. This is a point well worthy of note: for the world hath abused itself at all times, by endeavouring to please God with trifles. Behold the *heathens!* they were sensible that they could not call upon God unless they had some mediator: they therefore had their intercessours, by which they devised a thousand ways to find favour with God. The papists endeavoured to please him by washing and purifying themselves; which was but an apish imitation of that which God had appointed the *fathers:* where he made use of these corruptible elements, to draw them to Jesus Christ. When they came to the temple of Jerusalem, the water was ready, even at the entrance, that every one might purify himself, and thus come near the majesty of God: but this remedy was not in the water, which was a corruptible element, but it was a figure of the blood of our Lord Jesus Christ.

Let us abuse ourselves no more, by thinking that we can purchase God's favour by any ceremony or trifle of our own; for we should have been cast off and utterly condemned, had it not been for the atonement made by the blood of Jesus Christ. Here our whole trust lieth, and by this we are assured that our sins are absolved. The papists say that original sin is forgiven us in baptism: and if there should be a Jew or Heathen baptised at the age of twenty, thirty, or forty years, the sins which he had committed during his life, would then be forgiven him: but if after we are baptised, we fall, and commit sin, we must not expect to find grace and pardon unless we bring some recompense.

The papists are constrained to confess that they cannot thoroughly recompense God as they ought, and that it is impossible for men to make payment to him in all things: therefore they add another supply; which is, the blood of martyrs, and the keys of the church; (the power given to priests.) Thus they destroy the ransom which was made for us by the death and suffering of our Lord Jesus, trusting in their own performances and works of supererogation; and if there be any thing wanting, the blood of martyrs, and the keys of the church, fill up the account. Behold what horrible blasphemy!

Doth St. Paul speak here of a ransom that was made for little children only, and for those that are not baptized? Nay, on the contrary, he comprehendeth all faults which make us guilty before God; for the way is open whereby we may come to him by prayer, and find mercy. The ransom of which St. Paul speaketh, reacheth to all our sins; we must therefore have recourse to it from day to day, and place all our confidence therein. It is not only in this place that holy writ directeth us to the death and passion of our Lord Jesus Christ, and to the shedding of his blood for the absolution of our sins, but this doctrine is common throughout the scripture.

Let us understand the necessity of a redeemer, and that by the price of his blood we are reconciled to God the Father, and have free access to him by prayer. St. Paul having shown us that the grace which was purchased by the Son of God, was common to all mankind, and that it was not confined to the Jews only, it might be asked, why God chose one certain people for his inheritance? why it was his pleasure that the Jews only should call upon him? why he shut up his promises among them? why he gave them figures, and exercised them with an expectation of this great redeemer that was promised? It is true, that from the creation of the world, God always reserved for himself some people: yea, and when he made his covenant with Abraham, he shut out the Heathen from the hope of salvation; although for a time it pleased him to use a special grace toward the Jews, yet this doth not prevent his calling all mankind at present: for it pleaseth him to make the Heathen and the Gentile partakers of it, and to have his church extend throughout the world, and to bring them to the fold, who were afar off. Thus we have the meaning of the apostle.

We may here notice, that it would have been of little use to us, for Jesus Christ to have made the atonement, unless we were certified of this benefit, and were told that God had called us to enter into possession of this salvation, and to enjoy the blessings which had been purchased for us. For example, behold the Turks, who cast away the grace which was purchased for all the world by Jesus Christ; the Jews do so likewise; and the papists, although they do it not so openly, show it in effect: all of whom are as much shut out, and banished from the redemption which was purchased for us, as if Jesus Christ had never come into the world. And why so? Because they have not this witness; *that Jesus Christ is their redeemer.* Although they have some little taste, yet they always remain starved; and if they hear the word *redeemer* mentioned, it bringeth no comfort to them; neither do they receive any benefit from what is contained in the gospel.

Thus we perceive that those who are not partakers of the blessings purchased by our Lord Jesus Christ, receive not the witness. Before Jesus Christ came into the world, the Gentiles were not only unbelievers, but God had blinded their eyes; insomuch that it seemed as if Christ came only for one certain people. Yea, one would have thought, in the time of the law, that God had not spread forth the knowledge of his truth over all the world, but had given it to a particular people, whom he held for his church.

St. Paul informeth us, that it pleased God to give his law to the *fathers,* and set them apart from the rest of the world: he testified his good will toward Israel, and not to other nations; as it is said, Psalms lxxiv. 20. "Have respect unto the covenant: for the dark places of the earth are full of the habitations of cruelty." Moses likewise saith, Deut. xxxii. 9. "For the Lord's portion is his people; Jacob is the lot of his inheritance." We see therefore that God chose for himself a particular people: namely, the stock of Abraham; setting others aside as strangers. This is true, saith St. Paul, but it is now necessary that this knowledge should be spread over all the world; to wit, That God is the Father and Saviour of the Gentiles, as well as the Jews.

We may therefore perceive that the death and passion of our Lord Jesus Christ would be unprofitable to us, unless it were witnessed by the gospel. For it is faith that putteth us in possession of this salvation. This is a very profitable doctrine : for it is acknowledged that the greatest benefits that can be bestowed upon man in this world, is to be partaker of the salvation purchased by Jesus Christ ; however, there are but few that take the right way to obtain it. For we see how the gospel is despised, and how men stop their ears against the voice which God hath ordered to be proclaimed throughout the world !

We see but few now-a-days that become reconciled to God by the death of Jesus Christ ; for they deprive themselves of this witness : others cast it away, or at least, profit so little by it, that Jesus Christ dwelleth not in them by faith, to make them partakers of his blessings. St. Paul saith, 1 Cor. i. 30. " But of him are ye in Christ Jesus, who of God is made unto us wisdom, and righteousness, and sanctification, and redemption :" that being grafted into him, we may have part and portion in all his riches ; and that whatsoever he hath, may be ours. Seeing he was once pleased to become our brother, we must not doubt, but that in taking upon him our poor and wretched state, he hath made an exchange with us, that we may become rich through his grace.

It is certain that God hath always borne witness of himself ; yea, even to the Heathens. Although they had neither law nor prophets, he hath declared himself to them sufficiently, to leave them without excuse. If there were nothing but the order of nature, (as St. Paul maketh mention, Acts xiv.) it would be sufficient to convince infidels of their unthankfulness to God, who formed them, and hath nourished them through life. For it is said in the xix Psalm, *The heavens declare the glory of God, and the firmament showeth his handy work :* although they speak not, yet they set forth his goodness in such a manner, that we ought to be convinced without any other instructer. Behold the book of nature ! written with letters plain enough to make known to us that we ought to glorify God!

But this witness was too dark for the rudeness and weakness of men : it was therefore necessary that God should reveal himself in another manner, which was far greater ; which he hath done by means of the gospel. The law and the prophets were as a lamp to lighten the Jews, but they belonged to but one people. But this grace is bestowed generally upon all the nations of the earth. Therefore, it is not without cause that St. Paul saith, this witness was *to be testified in due time.*

In another place, we see how marvellously he setteth forth this great secret, which God had kept from the beginning of the world, but had now revealed by the preaching of the gospel ; insomuch, saith he, that the angels marvel at it : to see those who were separated from God, who seemed to be cut off and banished from salvation, now taken for his children, to be members of Jesus Christ, and of the fellowship and company of angels. This was a wonderful secret, and enough to astonish all creatures ! St. Paul saith, Gal. iv. 4 and 5. "But when the fulness of the time was come, God sent forth his Son, made of a woman, made under the law, to redeem them that were under the law, that we might receive the adoption of sons." Wherein it pleased him to make known to the world, that which was before unknown to the *fathers.*

For he saith, Eph. ii. 12, 13, 14, 15. "That at that time ye were without Christ, being aliens from the commonwealth of Israel, and strangers from the covenants of promise, having no hope, and without God in the world : but now, in Christ Jesus, ye, who sometime were far off, are made nigh by the blood of Christ. For he is our peace, who hath made both one, and hath broken down the middle wall of partition between us ; having abolished in his flesh the enmity, even the law of commandments contained in ordinances, for to make in himself of twain one new man, so making peace." Thus, the discord which was between the Jews and Gentiles was abolished.

Jesus Christ hath not only proclaimed the glad tidings, but hath sent forth his apostles and ministers to preach and publish peace to the world : to assemble the Jews, who were nigh by reason of the covenant, and by the solemn pledge made to their fathers, but who still needed a reconciliation through Jesus Christ the redeemer. These glad tidings were afterwards directed to those who were afar off; even to the poor Gentiles : they also received the message of salvation, and the peace of God; being assured that God so loved them, that he forgave all their sins. Thus the partition wall was broken down, and the ceremonies destroyed, whereby God had made a difference between the Jews and the Gentiles. And why so? Because this salvation belongeth to all the world without exception.

We therefore have this doctrine made clear; namely, that it was requisite for our Lord Jesus Christ to make an atonement for our sins ; and that by his death he hath purchased our redemption. We must therefore come to the testimony set forth in the gospel, that we may enjoy the blessings contained therein. We must not say that God is changeable, because it pleased him to hide the witness of his gospel from the Gentiles for a season, and afterwards to have it preached throughout the world, for this he had determined in the counsel of his own will. Let us therefore be convinced that it is our duty to worship and reverence him with all humbleness, for this is the greatest wisdom we can possess.

We must not be too curious in seeking vain and unprofitable questions : for God, who knoweth what we are able to bear, hath made known that which is proper for us to understand : let us therefore learn in his school, and no where else. Isaiah speaketh of *an acceptable time*, chap. xlix. 8. He calleth it an acceptable time, when the message of salvation is carried throughout all the world. Seeing then that God hath displayed his goodness, and showeth that he chose a particular time to call us to salvation, let us not on our part be stiff-necked, and show our corrupt hearts, and say all is not well, for this churlishness will prevent our coming to God; but let us heartily content and rest ourselves upon the grace offered, that there may be a sweet union between God and us; and that we may acknowledge it to be a fit time, because the Lord hath chosen it.

If things do not go according to our own minds, we must not find fault, and say, God should have done otherwise, but let us restrain ourselves, and show implicit obedience to his divine will ; let us be ruled by his counsel, and remember that it is not for us to appoint a time when he shall do what is to be done: this mastership and office of commanding is not in our hands, but belongs to God alone. When the gospel is called a witness, it is to assure us that God is kind and favourable toward us ; but if we doubt, after having this assurance of his good will, and stand wavering, and show ourselves rebellious against him, we cannot do him a greater dishonour. Let us remember that whenever the gospel is preached to us, God beareth us witness of his goodness.

Moreover, although they that speak to us be mortal men, yet let us consider in what situation God hath placed them; he hath made them his witnesses. When a man is sworn as a notary in any place, all the writings which he receiveth must be taken for true and authentical : if magistrates, who have so little authority, can do this, and the order be good and allowable in a commonwealth, how much more ought we, when God sendeth his witnesses to proclaim the gospel, to receive the message of salvation which they bring. If we do not, the honour of God is shamefully abused. Let us learn therefore to be more obedient than we have been in times past, and attend more strictly to the doctrine of the gospel.

If St. Paul was driven to fight against the pride and malice of men in his time, what is to be done now? for we see that ungodliness overfloweth, and the papists endeavour to abolish the remembrance of God's truth from the world. But we need not go so far; many among ourselves are profane, and tread the word of God, as it were, under foot: yea, and live in defiance of it. We see men who call themselves christians, and wish to be taken for such, yet they will not be governed by the word of God, but scorn and scoff at the doctrine of the gospel; I would to God these things were not so common among us.

If these scoffers come to hear a sermon once a month, it is to ascertain whether we speak according to their own fancy or not: if not, they immediately begin to murmur; and to say, all is nought; you would make us believe that we do not our duty! But let us mark well the words of St. Paul, where he protesteth that he is God's witness, and showeth that all who rebel against the gospel, and will not submit themselves to it, must not think that they have to deal with men, but with God; for the work is his. Let us therefore beware that we submit ourselves to God, and bow down our necks to his obedience; and so honour and magnify his glorious name, that he may acknowledge us as his children; that we may, all the days of our life, call upon him as our Father, and our Saviour!

THE END.

OTHER PURITAN TITLES
FROM SOLID GROUND BOOKS

In addition to *Selected Sermons from the Pastoral Epistles* printed here, Solid Ground has reprinted the following Puritan titles:

THE WORKS OF THOMAS MANTON - 22 Volumes
The Baptist Confession of Faith and Catechism - Leather Bound
A Body of Divinity by James Ussher
A Christian's Present for All Seasons: Thoughts of Eminent Divines
The Christian Warfare by John Downame
Classic Puritan NT Commentary by John Trapp
Commentary on Hebrews by William Gouge, 2 Volumes
Commentary on Second Peter by Thomas Adams
The Communicant's Companion by Matthew Henry
Exposition of the Baptist Catechism by Benjamin Beddome
Exposition of the Epistle of Jude by William Jenkyn
Exposition of the Ten Commandments by Ezekiel Hopkins
Farewell Sermons by Baxter, Brooks, Goodwin, Manton and more
Gospel Sonnets by Ralph Erskine
The Harmony of the Divine Attributes by William Bates
Heaven Upon Earth: Jesus, Best Friend in Worst Times by Janeway
The Marrow of True Justification by Benjamin Keach
The Redeemer's Tears Wept Over the Lost by John Howe
The Secret of Communion with God by Matthew Henry
A Short Explanation of Hebrews by David Dickson
The Three Forms of Unity – Leather Bound Edition
The Travels of True Godliness by Benjamin Keach

Call us at 205-443-0311
Visit our web site at soild-ground-books.com

www.ingramcontent.com/pod-product-compliance
Lightning Source LLC
Chambersburg PA
CBHW031143160426
43193CB00008B/238